Finding the Plot

Preaching in a Narrative Style

Roger Standing

WIPF & STOCK · Eugene, Oregon

Wipf and Stock Publishers
199 W 8th Ave, Suite 3
Eugene, OR 97401

Finding the Plot
Preaching in a Narrative Style
By Standing, Roger
Copyright©2004 by Standing, Roger
ISBN 13: 978-62032-031-0
Publication date 10/1/2012
Previously published by Paternoster, 2004

Contents

For Marion

who has listened to more of my sermons than anyone else, just as her father predicted. She has patiently advised, rebuked and encouraged me along the way and amazes me by not tiring of hearing my voice. I am a better preacher for her wisdom and **counsel**. I am a better person because of her love and friendship.

Preface

Eight years on since *Finding The Plot* was published in 2004, I am as convinced as ever of the importance of an understanding of narrative and plot development for Christian preachers. Since 2007 I have been part of the team at Spurgeon's College in London where we train men and women for Christian ministry. One of the special delights of this role is seeing those in the early days of their preaching ministry begin to experiment with the dynamics of preaching in a narrative style. To witness them developing skills that enable God's Word come alive in new ways with fresh life and texture is amazing.

While almost all of the text of the book remains the same as when it was first published, Chapter 12 which explores published and online resources has been thoroughly revised and updated. Recent years in the UK have seen a renaissance of interest in homiletics with an accompanying surge in conferences and published books and articles. In the USA, the high level of commitment to preaching has been maintained across the board. This flourishing of homiletical reflection is represented in the books, websites and organisations that are identified in this chapter.

While narrative preaching is not the 'be all and end all' of preaching, it gives a preacher another option to consider as they prepare to deliver God's Word, while an understanding of narrative and plot has the potential to enhance every sermon, whether from the telling of a personal anecdote, or the interpretation of the biblical narrative itself.

Roger Standing
London, Easter 2012

Introduction

I will always remember my first preaching engagement. I was sixteen years old. I had become a Christian the year before and was beginning to experience God's call to Christian service. I was passionate about my new found faith and wanted to share it at every possible opportunity. My minister, a godly man, presented with a teenager experiencing 'God's call', guided me towards preaching as a way to prepare for what lay ahead. So I found myself on a Sunday afternoon in January in one of Norfolk's large number of small rural chapels. Almost all of the twenty members were there. Sitting among the congregation were three accomplished lay preachers who looked on encouragingly. These were older men of spiritual stature and reputation.

I had thought about what I was going to say and had prayed that God would give me the words. Confidently I climbed the pulpit steps. Seven minutes later I was on my way back down. I had given my opening illustration and said a few words before almost drying up. I therefore repeated the illustration, retold the Bible story from the passage in Acts that I was using and then brought the sermon to a close. It had not gone well. I felt embarrassed. I wanted **the chapel floor to open up and swallow me. The wise** senior preacher who was acting as my guide said sagely,

'Son, if you'd gone up those steps like you came down; you'd have come down like you went up!'

I learned some important lessons that Sunday afternoon and there was a swift realisation that being the best that I could be entailed rather more than I had anticipated. Preaching the gospel of Jesus Christ was not merely standing up to share a few insights that had come through reading Scripture and prayerful reflection. It was an altogether more serious and demanding enterprise.

Over twenty-five years later I remain passionate about communicating the gospel. The preaching task remains a demanding one. Demanding, not only for the spiritual disciplines that it requires, but also because of the contemporary context in which it must be exercised.

In popular culture there have for a long time been two stereotypical views of preachers and their sermons. For a start, whether it is Homer Simpson falling asleep during the Rev Lovejoy's sermons in Springfield, or Alec Guinness' portrayal of mind-numbingly dull Canon d'Ascoyne in the 1949 Ealing Comedy, *Kind Hearts and Coronets*, the message is still the same, sermons are boring. At the other end of the scale are preachers who are full of life and emotional intensity, orators who know how to work a crowd and increase the size of the offering. Typified by Burt Lancaster as Elmer Gantry in the classic 1960 movie of the same name and Steve Martin playing revivalist Jonas Nightingale in *Leap of Faith*, these preachers are clearly on the make and are only in it for what they can get. Unfortunately, both of these stereotypes are sometimes true. Boring sermons are far from infrequent and the media are always keen to highlight the moral failure of a Jim Bakker or Jimmy Swaggart.

Such dim views of preaching are further heightened by the 'don't preach at me' philosophy of contemporary culture. This jibe expresses the popular distaste with moralising of any kind. The practice of preaching is typified as the prime example of such bad behaviour and is summarily written off. According to this received wisdom no one should be told what to do by another person. Each of us should construct our own set of values, belief system and the morality that flows out of them. Who needs or wants a preacher?

On top of this, we live in age, in the West, that has given rise to the most sophisticated set of listeners in the history of the world, even though they have the shortest ever attention span. Those in the media use an array of audio and visual techniques to enhance their programmes and messages. Advertisers spend billions of pounds every year with the expectation that their catchphrase will stick and that, as a result, people will go out and buy a product they recognise. What hope is there for a preacher standing before a congregation? **Against the background of modern communication** techniques, the creative demands on a local minister to write at least one new sermon most weeks are immense.

For all of the above reasons it is therefore no wonder that preaching is perceived by many to be dead in the water. But they are wrong. Every Sunday alone at least one preaching event happens in each of the 48,000 churches in the UK, not to mention the three hundred thousand places of worship in the USA. For all of the obituaries that have been written about the death of preaching, and for all the doom-laden prophecies of its demise, it still remains at the heart of the life of the Christian community.

This book is not written as an answer to the problems that are perceived to confront the gospel preacher in today's world; rather, it is written as a potential resource for those engaged in the demanding enterprise of contemporary preaching. It is a book that explores a potentially different style of preaching rather than seeking to alter its core content. In the process, I will argue that using a narrative style is not only an appropriate way to open the Scriptures for a congregation, but that it is also an approach particularly sensitive to the twenty-first century culture in which we live.

Adopting a narrative style is potentially an effective tool to enable us to communicate well with our hearers. It involves a completely different perspective on how to conceive, structure and deliver a sermon. It can allow the biblical story to come alive for the listener in fresh and exciting ways, which is something that a more traditional expository or topical approach rarely achieves. But, as will become clear, it is not merely telling stories.

Concentrating so much on the style of preaching has its pitfalls. One could easily become involved in what is merely an exercise in developing homiletical technique that undermines the real spiritual basis upon which preaching should stand, leaving a preacher more dependent upon human wit than the power of God. However, it is sobering to remember that just by preparing and preaching any sermon every preacher adopts a style. We may do it consciously, by following the example of a respected minister, or unconsciously, by just doing what comes naturally and easily.

In this book I outline how central the concept of narrative is to our culture, as well as to the biblical record itself. In turn, I examine how narrative works, the different forms a sermon may take to utilise these insights in communication and how a preacher might go about researching, writing and preaching in a different way. Finally, there are practical examples of sermons in the various narrative styles and the experiences of preachers from the UK and USA who have begun to explore this new style of preaching for themselves.

With such a narrowly defined objective there is a danger that some of the theological and spiritual assumptions upon which the practice of preaching is based, will, of necessity, remain unsaid. It is therefore appropriate, by way of the introduction of the subject, to sketch some of these underlying assumptions here.

While there are many things that might be included in such an outline, there are five interrelated theological principles that are pre-eminent, or even foundational, because they all touch on, and are formative for, our understanding of what Christian preaching is and our practice of preaching as disciples of Jesus.

The Primacy of Preaching: The Missiological Imperative

First, we must recognise and own the primacy of preaching itself in the Christian mission. It is at the heart of the ministry of Jesus and the task he entrusted his disciples to continue. It would not be an understatement to talk in theological terms of the missiological imperative of preaching. Luke leaves us in no doubt that this was Jesus' own self-understanding as he retells the events surrounding the early Galilean ministry and what some have called Jesus' 'manifesto sermon' at Nazareth in Luke 4:16–44. Quoting the prophet Isaiah, Jesus announces that the Spirit of the Lord has anointed him to 'preach good news to the poor ... and proclaim the year of the Lord's favour' (vv. 18–19). He identifies himself as a prophet (v. 24) and later, following his successful ministry in Capernaum, Jesus explains to the people why he must move on: 'I must preach the good news of the kingdom of God to the other towns also, because that is why I was sent' (v. 43).

The New Testament tells us that the apostles were trained and commissioned by Jesus to continue this preaching task (Mk. 3:14; Lk. 9:2; Acts 10:42), a task that Paul spells out to the church at Rome, lest anyone be in any doubt:

How, then, can they call on the one they have not believed in?
And how can they believe in the one of whom they have not
heard? And how can they hear without someone preaching to
them? And how can they preach unless they are sent? As it is
written, 'How beautiful are the feet of those who bring good
news!'

(Rom. 10:14–15)

The mission of Jesus has not changed. Preaching the good
news of the kingdom of God remains the primary responsibility of his church. Men and women are still called by God
to this task and are sent in his name to speak his word. This
sense of 'calling' is a very significant part of the spiritual
dimension of preaching.

For some, the sense of call from God comes in a more dramatic manner, like Paul's conversion and commission to
preach on the road to Damascus (Acts 26:16–20). My call
to preach was a remarkable experience. One night I was
praying in our flat and two Scripture references popped into
my mind – Acts 10:17 and 16:10. I had no idea what they
were, so I jotted them down and looked them up. It took my
breath away I realised their similarity. In the first, Peter had
just received the vision from God that leads him to preach to
Cornelius and his household. In the second, Paul has just
had the vision that results in his mission team crossing over
to Macedonia on a preaching and church planting expedi-
tion. I went to talk it through with my spiritual mentor and
counsellor, an older lady called Rita, convinced that I was
on the brink of having many visions! She refocused my
attention on the passages and the fact that the outcome of
Peter and Paul's prayerful devotion was to preach the gospel. 'This is the Lord's confirmation of his call on your life
to be a preacher,' she said. I can still hear her words now, all
these years later.

For others, the call comes in a different way, very often with the recognition of the need for people to speak God's word. Like Isaiah of old they hear the voice of the Lord saying, 'Whom shall I send? And who will go for us?' And they respond, 'Here am I. Send me' (Isa. 6:8). I once had a student minister working with me in the church I was pastoring in South London. He had no blinding flashes or dramatic spiritual encounters, but just the growing conviction that God was calling him to the ministry and preaching. His story may have been less dramatic, but it was no less spiritual. No one doubted that God's hand was on his life. That confirmation by God's people of our sense of calling and the accompanying gifting is not insignificant. It protects us from self-deceit and Christ's church from people being in the pulpit whose time and gifts would be better deployed elsewhere.

Preaching the Word of God: The Biblical Word

If the first foundational principle has to do with the primacy of preaching, the second has to address the content of our preaching. What is it that we are supposed to preach about?

In this age of entertainment those who can tell a good story well laced with humour will go far. But the biblical understanding of preaching is a long way from the Bible verse, anecdote, funny story model that captivates the imagination of many audiences. While a congregation may chuckle and enjoy themselves, this is little more than spiritualised stand up comedy. Neither is preaching the opportunity for a preacher to stand up and use the opportunity to parade their personal insights, wisdom, passions and prejudices. However well these may be dressed up in religious and spiritual language or more or less conveniently hung on some bible reference for justification, the biblical text has become merely a pretext for something else. Preaching is not even the medium by which we share our spiritual insights and intuitions because the core content of preaching lies elsewhere.

When I was a young preacher working in Liverpool as an evangelist, there was a Spaniard in the church; he came to the UK to work in the big Ford motor plant at Halewood. Luis learned to speak English with a Scouse accent. He was always a great encourager and constantly reminded me that I must always 'preacha da werd!' But what does it mean to preach the word of God? Actually, it means that we must be centred on Jesus who is the Word of God who became flesh and dwelt among us. The kingdom of God has come near to us in him. Of course, the only way we can access his heart and teaching is through the pages of the Bible, the written word of God, and especially through the New Testament. In fact, there is no other way in which we can begin to understand the message of Jesus. It is the only source we have. All of our preaching must be measured against the Bible and the truth it contains. As preachers we can never get past this.

While preaching may have many forms and styles, every Christian preacher has to be a student of the Bible. Every preacher must wrestle with the text to understand what it means. The insights of Bible commentators, other writers and preachers and the teaching of the church through the ages are all essential aids to helping us understand the revelation of God which the Bible contains. The eighteenth **century founder of Methodism,** John Wesley, claimed to be 'a man of one book'. By this he did not mean that he only read the Bible, but rather that all his reading was to the end that he understood the message of the gospel that it contained more adequately.

Christian preaching will always be thoroughly biblical. Its shape and form may vary, as may all the other constituent parts, but it will never depart from its foundational dependence upon the truth contained in the written word of God, the Bible. If it does, whatever else it may be, it is not Christian preaching. Good preaching will always contain humour, the personal experience and insight of the preacher and something of their convictions and passion. Yet it must never move beyond that which can be tested by Scripture.

The apostle Paul faced a dilemma. In his preaching he felt the pull of two very different audiences. On the one side were those within the Jewish community among whom he had grown up. They particularly wanted to hear about miraculous signs and wonders. On the other were those steeped in the Greek culture of the Roman Empire. They thrived on rational argument and intellectual stimulation. Yet Paul knew what the centre of his preaching was to be: 'Jews demand miraculous signs and Greeks look for wisdom, but we preach Christ crucified: a stumbling block to Jews and foolishness to Gentiles' (1 Cor. 1:22–23).

Truth Through Personality: The Incarnate Word

The third foundational principle is concerned with how God has chosen to relate with the world since the coming of Jesus. John makes this clear at the beginning of his Gospel:

> In the beginning was the Word, and the Word was with God, and the Word was God. He was with God in the beginning. Through him all things were made; without him nothing was made that has been made. In him was life, and that life was the light of men ... The Word became flesh and made his dwelling among us.
>
> (Jn. 1:1–4, 14)

When God set out to accomplish his purposes he did not send us a systematic theology to help us understand what to do. Rather, he chose for his Word to be fleshed out in a real life, in a real person. Not only was God's message communicated in words, it was also lived out through Jesus' life and work. His hearers could see what it looked like. It was tangible; the kingdom of God was at hand. Understood theologically as the incarnation, this is one of the New Testament's fundamental doctrines.

Following his death and resurrection, Jesus commissions his disciples to carry on his mission. He says, 'As the Father has sent me, I am sending you' (Jn. 20:21). This begs the question, 'How did the Father send the Son?' The answer is straightforward, by incarnation. Just as Jesus, the Word of God, needed human substance to communicate the good news of the gospel, so the same holds true for the preached word of God in our generation. It takes flesh and is proclaimed through the words of the preacher, guided and informed by character, experience and insight. In the much quoted words of Phillips Brooks:

> Truth through personality is our description of real preaching. The truth must come really through the person, not merely over his lips, not merely into his understanding and out through his pen. It must come through his character, his affections, his whole intelligence and study.[1]

This means that there has to be correspondence between the message and values of the gospel and the preacher's lifestyle. Jesus warns his disciples to be careful not to fall into the trap of the Pharisees and teachers of the law who did not practice what they preached (Mt. 23:3). Paul, when opening his heart to the Corinthian church, speaks about the

---

[1] Phillips Brooks, *Eight Lectures on Preaching*, 8.

rigorous regime of discipline he placed himself under to ensure that he did not disqualify himself having preached to others (1 Cor. 9:26–27). Elsewhere, Paul points out to Timothy, the younger leader, the relationship between what a preacher says and what a preacher does. He counsels him to keep a close watch on his lifestyle and to look to be a role model in how he speaks and conducts himself for those who listen to him (1 Tim. 4:12–16). According to James, those who presume to undertake a teaching role in the church are judged more strictly (Jas. 3:1).

Previous generations to ours would have talked about the personal holiness of the preacher and the need to have clean hands and a pure heart to stand in the holy place and preach the word of God (Ps. 24:3–6). Of course, there is nothing more odious than self-righteousness, that intense pursuit of the outward form of religion that misses its heart. Genuine righteousness follows a different line. An old saint once told me to always remember that, 'The closer you get to the Lord, the more you will find yourself on your knees.' The more intimate our walk with Christ, the greater our recognition of our need for his grace in all things. This brings a gentleness and humility of spirit that has a burning passion for others to know and share the riches of his grace:

> O that the world might taste and see
> The riches of his grace!
> The arms of love that compass me
> Would all mankind embrace …
> Preach him to all, and cry in death:
> 'Behold, behold the Lamb!'[2]

---

[2] Charles Wesley, from the hymn, 'Jesus – the name high over all'.

Audience Focused: The Contextualised Word

The fourth foundational principle is closely related to the incarnation. Indeed, it is a consequence of it. When the Word of God became flesh and dwelt among us he was an historical person. He lived a real life, in the real world, at a specific point in history. Profoundly influenced by Hellenism, Alexander the Great and Rome, Jesus' natural tongue would have been Aramaic. He was also able to read the Jewish scriptures in Hebrew and, having ministered in the Decapolis (Mk. 7:31), it is highly likely that he spoke Greek. In addition, there is the probability that he also understood the administrative language of the Roman Empire, Latin. He knew the cosmopolitan life of Galilee and the nature of living in a state that had lost its autonomy to an occupying military power. These influences would have been in sharp relief for him having established Capernaum as the centre for his early ministry (Mt. 4:13). The city was situated on a provincial border, and a custom post on the *Via Maris* trade route was also located there with a resident Roman garrison.

This is about context. Jesus lived and ministered in a specific place at a specific time. A brief survey of the preaching material he uses goes to illustrate how this context was determinative for his ministry. He used culturally appropriate metaphors and analogies as illustrative aids in his speaking. He spoke about what people knew, and used that as a means to open up the truth of God to his hearers. For example, he used insights gleaned from agriculture (Mt. 9:35–38, 13:1–43), the countryside (Mt. 5:25–34), the construction industry (Mt. 7:24–29), and the cultural rites of passage in family life (Mt. 22:1–14). On other occasions, he picked up on social prejudices (Lk. 10:25–37), social customs (Lk. 15:8–10), personal relationships (Lk .15:11–31), the experience of management (Lk. 16:1–15) and of casual labour (Mt. 20:1–16).

Originally, it was those involved in cross-cultural mission that saw the importance of incarnating the gospel fully into the language, customs and traditions of cultures different to their own. They called this process contextualisation. David Bosch believes that if the incarnation is taken seriously the Word must become flesh in every new context.[3] While most preachers may not be involved in the kind of cross-cultural work experienced by those who travel overseas, still there are important lessons to be learned. Who are we seeking to communicate the gospel with when we preach? Even in our own community there are many cultural differences. How we would communicate with a congregation that had an older age profile would differ dramatically to a presentation on the same biblical story at a youth event. There are many differences in the nuances of culture between these poles of age. Similarly, there are many different cultural identities we could highlight like education, ethnicity, churched or unchurched, regional variations and occupation or social class. Contextualisation is about the audience, group or congregation that a preacher is to address. How should the sermon be constructed to enable those who are listening to most adequately hear what is being proclaimed?

Collaboration with the Holy Spirit: The Inspired Word

The fifth foundational principle for preaching is rooted in the Christian belief that God is neither distant nor aloof

---

[3] David Bosch, *Transforming Mission: Paradigm Shifts in Theology of Mission*, 21.

from his world. His presence not only pervades creation (his immanence), but he also seeks to live in relationship with that which he has created. The fact that Jesus is identified as the Word of God underlines the divine predisposition to communicate with people. As a consequence, it is no surprise to see how highly the New Testament values the task. In preaching God's truth can again be revealed to the world. By it believers also have a significant means by which to hear the voice of God for themselves. It is no coincidence that in the lead up to hundreds of thousands of preaching services each Sunday godly women and men pray that God will speak to his people.

Preaching is more than just a religious speech, based on thorough research and carefully crafted words. However good such an exercise in communication this might be, it is not biblical preaching. There is a spiritual dimension that cannot be overlooked. In the New Testament there is a clear connection between the practice of preaching and the Holy Spirit, God's active presence in the world. Speaking to his disciples of what lies ahead and how they are to give an account of the gospel they know to be true, Jesus instructs them: 'do not worry about what to say or how to say it. At that time you will be given what to say, for it will not be you speaking, but the Spirit of your Father speaking through you' (Mt. 10:19–20).

Prior to his crucifixion, Jesus seeks to further make clear to the disciples the importance of the work of the Holy Spirit in their coming mission. He, the Holy Spirit, will be the one who 'will convict the world of guilt in regard to sin and righteousness and judgment' (Jn. 16:8). He will be their teacher guiding them into all the truth. He will be the one who is the active go-between who connects heaven and earth by making known the heart and mind of God' (Jn. 16:7–14). After his resurrection, Jesus again stresses the indispensable role the Holy Spirit will have in the disciples' forthcoming mission by instructing them to remain in Jerusalem until they receive a special outpouring of power from the Holy Spirit. The Spirit comes on the day of Pentecost and the first thing that Peter does is to preach a sermon (Lk. 24:49; Acts 1:8; 2:14–40). In his first letter, Peter gives an insight into how he understood the ministry of preaching. He speaks of those 'who have preached the gospel to you by the Holy Spirit sent from heaven' (1 Pet. 1:12).

This has direct implications for the preacher as biblical preaching is inextricably linked to the vitality of their own spiritual life. It is a collaborative task shared with the Holy Spirit who both guides the preparation and empowers the preaching. Should a preacher's spiritual discernment be dulled or compromised there is no way of avoiding a direct impact on the preaching itself.

If God's heart is to communicate with people, the basic question a preacher must ask is 'What does God want me to say?' As Haddon Robinson points out, 'a preacher must learn to listen to God before he speaks for him'.[4]

Various elements come together in this process of discernment:

- Studying the Scriptures.
- Discovering what others have said or written about a given passage or subject.
- Understanding who will be listening to the sermon and what makes them who they are.
- Prayer that immerses the whole process of preparation with the questions, 'Is this what you want me to say and how you want me to say it?'

---

[4] Haddon W. Robinson, *Biblical Preaching: The Development and Delivery of Expository Messages*, 26.

Thus the preacher becomes a partner with the Holy Spirit, acting on the divine predisposition to communicate.

Yet it is a sobering experience to be caught up by God in the ministry of preaching. When all the communications seminars have been completed and every book on homiletical practice consumed, God will still be God. You would think it was important to speak the right word at the right time, yet a seasoned old preacher once said to me, echoing the words of 2 Timothy 4:2, 'Roger, there are only two occasions on which you are to preach the gospel – in season and out of season!' The apostle Paul too, surprisingly, does not seem to mind what a preacher's motives are, whether they are good or false, only that Christ is preached (Phil. 1:15–18). Indeed, as we have already seen, he reminds the church at Corinth that the message of Christianity is ultimately viewed by the world as sheer foolishness. In that sense, a preacher can never depend upon wise and persuasive words, but for a spiritual encounter to result from the preached word of God, the preacher must be dependent upon the Spirit's power (1 Cor. 1:18–24; 2:4–5). Charles Haddon Spurgeon, the great Victorian Baptist preacher, recounts that it was among a despised people in an insignificant chapel of a peculiar sect that:

> The preacher read that precious text: 'Look unto me, and be ye saved, all the ends of the earth; for I am God, and beside me there is none else'; and as I thought, fixing his eyes on me, before he began to preach to others, he said: 'Young man! Look! Look! Look!'

And so the great preacher came to faith. However, saying that we are depending upon the Spirit's power can become an easy excuse to allow us to sidestep the need for study and preparation that helps us to be the very best we can be in our preaching for the Lord. Lest we fall into this error of spiritualised laziness, consider Paul's advice to Timothy: 'Let the elders who rule well be considered worthy of double honor, especially those who work hard at preaching and teaching' (1 Tim 5:17 NAS).

My hope is that this book will be of assistance to you as you work hard at your preaching and teaching.

Part 1

What's So Special About Narrative?

1

The World Changed

On 1 August 1981 a little known British pop group appeared as the first act on a newly born American television station. MTV was to become a cultural trend-setter for the rest of the century, shaping the world of the rising generation. As the videotape began to roll those first viewers were treated to The Buggles singing their prophetic contribution to pop culture, 'Video killed the radio star'. Having reached the top of the UK charts in October 1979 it had not been a huge hit in the United States. Yet *Billboard Magazine* rated it as a sort of anthem for late 1970s living. The lyrics about the power of video compared to the radio were telling.

Whatever the impact of pop videos on contemporary youth culture, the moving pictures of TV had already been credited with a rapid decline in attendance at Sunday evening church services in the UK. In 1967 the BBC screened its adaptation of John Galworthy's, *The Forsyte Saga*. The last major British serial to be filmed in black and white, the twenty-six episodes attracted an audience of six million each Sunday evening. This was an amazing number for the minority interest channel, BBC 2. However, when it was repeated the following year on BBC 1 a staggering eighteen million viewers tuned in each week, or almost half the adults in the country.

The Forsyte Saga and MTV symbolize the way the
world changed during the twentieth century, altering forever the context in which our preaching takes place. The
last one hundred years have seen western society living in
revolutionary times so far as communication is concerned.
Analysing this trend and its implications for the church Rob
Warner observes that, 'as the TV revolution not merely continues to unfold but accelerates, the tragic truth in many
churches is that with every passing year God and the gospel
are more firmly gagged and bound'.[1]

Gagged and bound in a time of unprecedented decline.
The figures for the UK speak for themselves. Take for example the decline in attendance at worship services. It has been
dramatic. A 13 per cent decline between the ten years
1979–89 accelerated to 22 per cent during the 1990s.
Indeed, the number of under–15's in church fell from 25 per
cent to 19 per cent, while only 5 per cent of twenty-
somethings attend worship in England.[2] The rapidity of this
fall has led many to ask serious questions regarding its
causes and how it can be reversed.

On one hand, many hold the nostalgic belief that, if they
only pray, wait faithfully, and remain true to the tradition
they received, the Lord will make tomorrow like yesterday
and the 'good old days' they remember. Others, recognising
that the world of the twenty-first century is a vastly different place from that of the late nineteenth and early
twentieth centuries, look for fundamental change to
address the new cultural context in which we live.

One of the most significant issues before us is how
do we communicate in an information saturated and
multimedia-enhanced culture? The present generation of

[1] Rob Warner, *21st Century Church: (Why Radical Change
Cannot Wait)*, 23.
[2] Peter Brierley, *UK Christian Handbook*, 0.3–0.4.

forty-somethings were weaned on television; those under forty continue to have increasingly sophisticated tastes as they consume electronic media through terrestrial, cable and digital TV, videos, CDs, DVDs and the Internet. It is hardly surprising therefore that the, 'It was boring,' critique of many a teenager following a church service was overwhelmingly substantiated in a survey conducted by Gallup in the UK. They found that the clear majority in every age group younger than fifty thought traditional church worship services were boring. Given that from Monday to Saturday we live in a world shaped by TV, failure to engage with the implications of this prevailing culture has serious consequences for our communication of the gospel. We may be literally boring people to hell.

Neil Postman outlines the reason for the boredom in his analysis of public debate in contemporary society. He charts how the 'age of exposition' has given way to the 'age of show business' as the role of the printing press in public discourse on politics, education, and religion has been displaced by the all-pervasive growth of TV. Consequently, public discourse 'has become shrivelled and absurd'.[3] With TV as the command centre of the new epistemology, all public understanding is coloured by its biases and must be communicated according to the new supra-ideology of entertainment.[4]

Social commentators have recognised two distinct subcultures that have been influenced by these trends having grown up in western society since the World War II: the 'Baby Boomers' and 'Generation X'. An increasing birth rate spawned the 'baby boom' (c.1946–64) and the birth of a generation that comprises roughly one-third of the

---

[3] Neil Postman, *Amusing Ourselves to Death: Public Discourse in the Age of Show Business*, 16.

[4] Postman, *Amusing*, 78, 87.

population. It has been typified as the first 'standardised generation' in the US with standardised kitchens in the 1940s, standardised school curricula in the 1950s and a standardised fear of nuclear holocaust from the 1960s. This is also a generation comfortable with change as it has been a normal part of their life experience. Because of its size, the Boomer generation has increasingly exercised a normative influence on society.

Wade Clark Roof in his analysis of the spiritual trends among Boomers observes that television has been central to their experience. They are the first generation to have grown up with it. It provided for them a unifying common experience that introduced the adult world at a very early age. Its impact has been profound, replacing word with image in communication and delivering a culture typified by instant gratification and immediacy. Seeing, not reading, is the Boomers' basis for believing.[5]

Roof also notes that Boomers are, 'deeply enmeshed in the narrative tradition – for at heart they are storytellers, and like all storytellers, they know that life is an open-ended plot'.[6] Choice is an integral part of life for this generation. Religiously this means a consumer mentality, which will take them where their needs are being met. How Boomers perceive the 'culture' of a congregation is highly significant as it determines how attractive that church is to them. Their concern is not so much its religious background, polity and social context as its 'worldview, plot, and identity ... [its] mood, atmosphere, tone, sight, tastes, and ... its own "style", its own set of encoded meanings about sacred realities'.[7]

---

[5] Wade C. Roof, *A Generation of Seekers: Public Discourse in the Age of Show Business*, 53–4.

[6] Roof, *Generation of Seekers*, 261.

[7] Roof, *Generation of Seekers*, 204.

Generation X[8] (c.1965–82) has adapted to a rapidly accelerating technological culture. History is happening much faster now. George Barna observes that change is barely perceptible to them. Living in a world that has radically reinvented itself every decade, it is the absence of change that would seem abnormal. Indeed, without change they would feel cheated of the joy of experiencing the new and creative, the novel and mysterious.[9]

'Xers' are the first wave of humanity to reach adulthood on the post-industrial side of the historical divide, and this has dramatic implications for them. Pre-eminent among these developments is the arrival of the 'information age.' The average Xer spends two to three hours a day watching TV and will consume eighty-nine movies in a year. Significantly, 38 per cent spend around a quarter of their TV time watching MTV. That is important because 'MTV-ivification' is a significant contributor to the shaping of the reduced attention spans and decrease in the boredom threshold that typifies this generation. MTV-style videos have edit cuts every three seconds and MTV-genre commercials are even faster.[10] In addition, even in the early 1990s Xers were spending an average of thirty to forty minutes on a personal computer (PC) each day. With the proliferation of PCs and increasing access to the Internet, it is fair to estimate that this is a very conservative figure. Barna concludes with a perceptive insight into the Generation X worldview when he remarks: 'Where older people see technology as a

---

[8] A term coined by Douglas Coupland in his novel of the same name. This group is also designated as 'Baby Busters' in relation to Baby Boomers.

[9] George Barna, *Generation Next: What You Need to Know About Today's Youth*, 110.

[10] Kevin G. Ford, *Jesus for a New Generation: Reaching Out to Today's Young Adults*, 55; Barna, *Generation Next*, 52–4.

tool to be harnessed ... [Xers] view technology as a means of expression to be unleashed.'[11]

Electronic media are destined to become ever more sophisticated and of increasing quality, with an explosion of variety and range of available product options. Twenty-first century films will be increasingly dominated by computer-generated virtual sequences that have been so successful in a variety movies such as the *Matrix* trilogy, *The Lord of the Rings* series and *Gladiator*. Multimedia rich presentations will be routine in the business world. Professional presentations, already replete with computer driven graphics, sound, video and video conferencing, will increasingly be judged not just by content but by the way the technology itself is used.

New generation TV, with its plasma screens, will not be exempt from radical change either. Audience scoping will provide instant analysis of how viewers are feeling, and interactive TV will replace patterns of passive viewing with participation in program content and delivery. The 500 channels soon to be available through digital broadcast techniques will be supplanted by the total choice of Internet TV. As technology improves it will provide instant access to 100,000 films starting right now at the push of a button or 300,000 popular programmes after a delay of less than twenty seconds, all of digital TV quality. In addition to these developments, any projection of the future must factor in the coming boom industry of virtual reality as this technology improves, becoming cheaper and more user-friendly.[12]

So, how far have TV and the multimedia mentality affected the context within which preaching is exercised?

---

[11] Barna, *Generation Next*, 115.
[12] Patrick Dixon, *Futurewise: Six Faces of Global Change*, 26–7, 34–5, 37, 98.

British media expert Malcolm Muggeridge believed that TV was the greatest single influence in society back in the late 1970s.[13] This has only increased over the ensuing decades, and perhaps accounts for Neil Postman's thesis that television has redefined the nature of public discourse. The practical impact of TV on audiences has been widely charted and in relation to traditional preaching the consequences are significant. Michael Rogness helpfully notes five of the most significant factors. These are that TV:

- conveys pictures rather than concepts.
- conveys information in bytes or impressions, rather than sequentially.
- has reduced the concentration span.
- causes passive listening.
- combines verbal and non-verbal communication.[14]

This multi-sense engagement of sight and sound engages both right and left brain function, it alters the way people process their thoughts, particularly by reducing the need for concentration and effort. Listening to a preacher can be hard work by comparison.

Timothy Turner also believes that these factors affect the mood of TV, which is casual and relaxed with a more direct appeal to the feelings rather than thinking. As a medium it is intimate, but impersonal, with the use of the teleprompt restoring the eye contact of oral communication while a prepared script is read. He sees a TV-conditioned mentality as constituting a real barrier to effective preaching because it has altered the mental skills and listening aptitudes of the audience. As a consequence, it requires less concentration

---

[13] Timothy A. Turner, *Preaching to Programmed People: Effective Communication in a Media-saturated Society*, 15.
[14] Michael Rogness, *Preaching to a TV Generation*, 24–31.

and effort and is far more entertaining. By comparison, a worship service with the use of the Bible is a far more serious and formal endeavour.[15] It is hardly surprising that the boredom threshold when listening to a sermon has substantially reduced over the years. Indeed, British preacher John Stott observes that the lengthy exposure of contemporary people to TV increases their, 'physical laziness, intellectual flabbiness, emotional exhaustion, psychological confusion and moral disorientation'.[16]

It is sobering to realise that estimates indicate people between the ages of 25 to 40 have watched an average of 30–40,000 hours of TV and some 250,000 advertisements. If our style of preaching is to be audience-focused it must be remembered that the staple diet of TV is the story, which heavily influences the whole viewing experience. Stories are everywhere. They are found in the daily ration of soap opera, the movie blockbuster, the mini-narratives of commercials, and the 'stories' in the nightly news. Indeed, TV audiences are hooked on the narrative principle of the movement from tension to resolution. It can be spotted in other programmes that are not so readily obvious. On chat shows celebrities bare their souls, share their experiences and so tell their stories. The audiences of reality-TV programmes become consumers of an unfolding narrative – who will win this series of *Pop Idol* or be the next to be evicted from the *Big Brother* House? The same principle also works in a number of highly successful game shows – for example, *Who Wants to be a Millionaire?*, where viewers hang on as the plot unravels to see whether this time will see the magical seven-figure cheque handed over.

---

[15]　Turner, *Programmed People*, 19–21, 33, 94–5.
[16]　John Stott, *Between Two Worlds: The Art of Preaching in the Twentieth Century*, 70–4.

If preaching does not take account of the world it addresses, it will be a means of communication foreign to those outside the church and increasingly alien to those inside it. Consequently, people will find sermons increasingly difficult to access and learn from. Our preaching has to take account of the realities of both contemporary culture and the prevailing trends in communication. If not, only those sermon listeners with sufficient tenure to have been adequately exposed to, and educated in, the genre will adequately benefit from it. To contemplate such things is **to begin to** engage with an activity that will involve potentially radical change for both preacher and congregation. However, to avoid these issues will deny access to the gospel for an increasingly large segment of society, because they are both alienated from the value and belief systems of the Judeo-Christian tradition and from the Church's means of communicating faith.

When the church attempts to meet these issues Thomas Troeger sees it as doing nothing that it has not also done throughout history. Rather, it is part of Christianity's 'infinite translatability' which always disturbs the orthodox when confronted by a new cultural milieu.[17] Unfortunately, the absence of change may be in part a contributor to the 'post-evangelical' drift out of evangelical churches in the UK noted by Dave Tomlinson, who coined the phrase. He relates, 'My thesis is simple: that post-evangelicals tend to be people who identify culturally more with postmodernity ... and that this has a significant bearing on the way that they approach and understand the Christian faith.'[18]

Entering into the post-evangelical debate, Maggie Dawn maintains that for the church to insist on continuity of

---

[17] Thomas Troeger, *Ten Strategies for Preaching in a Multimedia Culture*, 8–9, 17.

[18] Dave Tomlinson, *The Post Evangelical*, 76.

language and form is cultural blindness. Culture changes: to keep Christianity stuck in a 'time warp' is to actually change its meaning. Yet she would want to draw a line between being fashionable and being relevant. Being fashionable merely dresses the gospel in contemporary cultural clothes. As such, culture is merely used rather than being engaged with at any depth.[19] Graham Cray concurs with her insights and states: 'In every era and society the Christian Church faces the challenge of contextualisation – ensuring that the gospel is being relevantly addressed to its culture from within, while avoiding syncretism.'[20]

It is because we live in the boundaries of the second great change in how we communicate with each other in the world that Richard Jensen sees that a change in our preaching is inevitable. Originally people communicated orally. Truth was conveyed in story form and it was the ear of the listener that was active. With the advent of writing and printing society became literate and the eye became the active organ as truth was distilled into a logical sequence of ideas. The post-literate age, typified by electronic communication, brings the ear back into play, but in a new way. Sight and sound are fused into a new medium. The language of the communicator has to re-embrace narrative and emotion, move from ideas to images and understand how the all-pervading use of stories makes a dramatic impact on both eye and ear. Communicators and preachers must now see themselves, at least in part, as dramatists, making the shift from thinking in ideas to thinking in story.[21]

So, what might preaching come to look like as the twenty-first century unfolds? In the United States Leith

---

[19] Maggie Dawn, 'You have to change to stay the same,' in Graham Cray (ed.), *The Post Evangelical Debate*, 41.
[20] Cray (ed.), *Post Evangelical Debate*, 2.
[21] Richard A. Jensen, *Thinking in Story*, 8–10, 53.

Anderson[22] identifies a number of different trends that must be taken into account as a result of contemporary cultural changes:

- a movement toward inductive narrative form from deductive outlined structures;
- relevance requiring local application for the life and community of the listeners at this point in time;
- multi-sense communication that uses video, drama, music and other sensory experiences;
- multi-layered presentations where different themes are woven throughout the fabric of a sermon;
- the development of a more conversational, chat show, communicator style as opposed to the orator, lecturer, preacher ethos of the past.

In the United Kingdom, Rob Warner identifies further significant changes relating to matters of style in communication. He perceives the most significant to be:

- a faster and snappier pace with rapid theme and mood changes;
- increased use of storytelling;
- decreasing dependence on linear flow of ideas;
- an increasing informality;
- increasing audience participation;
- increasing visual impact. [23]

Looking at the philosophical changes in contemporary society, Andrew Walker explores the increasing impact of postmodernism on the presentation of the gospel. He

---

[22] Leith Anderson, *A Church for the 21st Century*, 44–6, 209–11.
[23] Warner, *21st Century Church*, 22.

maintains that in the rediscovery of story and narrative, Christianity has an antidote that addresses the new cultural context caused by the rise of postmodernity and hegemony of television. Writing from the Eastern Orthodox tradition, he sees narrative as about discovering those images which enhance the word and set the story in colour and space, acting as windows to heaven.

There is nothing new about storytelling and the power of a narrative to hold an audience. From the oldest civilizations that told community stories around the campfire to our own family stories that are handed down from generation to generation, stories have been important. While they have never gone out of fashion, only recently have they taken on a new ascendancy. Andrew Walker calls this reintroduction of oral culture and the return to the dominance of image the 'second orality'.[24] For Jensen it is the 're-oralisation' of post-literate culture by electronic communication. He sees 1985 as a landmark year in the United States as that was the year when more videos were rented from video stores than books were borrowed from libraries.[25] *The New York Times* quoted figures that substantiate this cultural shift in 1997. In 1996 the average American spent 100 hours reading books against 1600 watching broadcast and cable TV.[26]

Opinion formers have always understood the power of narrative to illustrate an issue by using a strategically placed anecdote or by deploying individuals to relate their personal experience. Drama has a long history of exploring issues in public debate, but the genre of docu-drama has

---

[24] Andrew Walker, *Telling the Story: Gospel, Mission and Culture*, 98.
[25] Jensen, *Thinking in Story*, 29, 49.
[26] *New York Times*, 24 August 1997.

seen a significant resurgence over recent years.[27] Among the most powerful have been the airing on the BBC of *The Day Britain Stopped* and the *If ...* series.[28]

Set in the near future *The Day Britain Stopped* took the form a documentary talking with politicians, emergency service personnel, eyewitnesses and members of the general public about the day when road, rail and air transport came to a stand still. Using a mixture of actors and individuals playing themselves it intentionally blurred the boundary between fact and fiction.

That our personal stories have always contributed to our sense of identity has always been true. Yet perceptions are changing. It's not just that our lives are our stories, but, as a character from Douglas Coupland's acclaimed novel, *Generation X*,[29] reflects, 'Either our lives become stories or there's just no way to get through them.' This cross-over is further heightened by the way in which the content of soap operas impacts viewers' lives. There must always have been the gullible few who believe that what they watch is actually real. However, Coupland makes another telling observation of how TV narratives increasingly define our social reality. In so doing he coined the term 'tele-parablising', that is, morals used in everyday life that derive from TV

---

[27] Out of vogue for many years docu-dramas are widely recognised to have their origins in Peter Watkin's *The War Game* of 1965. Originally banned by the BBC it won an Oscar for Best Documentary in 1967. *Smallpox 2002* saw the beginning of their rise in popularity.

[28] *The Day Britain Stopped* was Broadcast on BBC 1, May 13, 2003; *If ... the lights go out*; *If ... things don't get better*; *If ... the generations fall out*; *If ... it was a woman's world* and *If ... we don't stop eating* were broadcast on BBC2 between 10 March and 7 April, 2004.

[29] Douglas Coupland, *Generation X*.

sitcom plots: 'That's just like the episode where Jan lost her glasses!'

Recognising the power of narrative in our contemporary culture is to begin to understand something very important about those with whom we seek to communicate to as preachers. Thomas Troeger sees it as part of our responsibility as communicators of the gospel to participate with a God who conquers by capturing human imagination. Clearly, there is a danger of such an enterprise degenerating into mere entertainment, but it has a loftier motivation that is both biblically attested and theologically sound. As Michael Rogness has so acutely put it, to preach in the same way as previous generations will be as effective a method of communication today as a jerky old black-and-white silent movie in a state of the art movie theatre with wide screen and Dolby Surround Sound.[30] The world has changed.

---

[30] Rogness, *TV Generation*, 12.

2

God Has Given Us A Book Full of Stories

One of my oldest memories of church is sitting at the front of the Methodist chapel we attended with all the other members of the Sunday school. The preacher would tell us a story and then we would sing before we went out to our classes. I've always loved singing and can picture us now bellowing forth the words of one of the small selection of hymns that we sang. The melody continues to ring in my ears.

> God has given us a book full of stories,
> Which was made for His people of old;
> It begins with the tale of a garden,
> And ends with the city of gold.[1]

As quaint as the recollection now seems and as sentimental as the words of the hymn sound, this week by week experience marks the beginning of my lifelong love affair with the stories in Scripture. I was fascinated with the tale of Zacchaeus shinning up a tree to catch a better view of Jesus. The story of David and Goliath appealed to the action hero in me and I imagined myself held aloft on the shoulders of

---

[1] Maria Matilda Penstone.

war-weary soldiers being cheered for a great victory. I was entranced by the annual retelling of the nativity and relieved when I didn't have to play the part of an angel! One year at infant school I got to play the part of Balthazar, the fabled third King who brought myrrh to the baby Jesus. I even got to sing on my own the appropriate verse of the famous Christmas Carol, 'We three kings of Orient are'.

While I've known all my life that the Bible is full of stories, it was a long time before I appreciated the significance. While the founding documents of the Christian religion could have been a systematic theology or a comprehensive book of law, thankfully they are not. God really has given us a book full of stories. If the Bible truly is God's book, then God must be a storyteller. Stories dominate the Bible. Indeed, Sidney Greidanus describes narrative as the, 'central, foundational, and all-encompassing genre of the Bible'.[2]

If you began to list the books of biblical narrative – for example, the Gospels, the Acts of the Apostles, the Pentateuch, the historical books of Samuel, Kings and Chronicles, Ezra-Nehemiah, Esther, Ruth, Job, Daniel ... – you would find that it is actually easier to name those biblical books that do not follow a narrative form. In addition, those books that are not primarily narrative, for example the Psalms, the epistles or the prophets are often only properly understood when their place in a wider narrative is appreciated. Indeed, in such books the narrative regularly surfaces in the text. In the letter to the Galatians Paul's interactions with Peter and the Jerusalem church are a particular focus (Gal. 1:11 – 2:14). In Psalm 51 David's misguided course of action with Uriah and Bathsheba issues in a profound expression of repentance.

---

[2] Sidney Greidanus, *The Modern Preacher and the Ancient Text: Interpreting and Preaching Biblical Literature*, 188.

Many scholars have sought to categorise the various literary genres found in the Bible. A brief overview demonstrates how pervasive the narrative style is.[3]

1. *Simple Reports* tend to be short and unembellished accounts of single events that concentrate on what actually happened. Most often they are told in the third person and range over a wide variety of topics. The different categories of simple reports include:

- *Personal anecdotes* from the life of an individual such as when Elisha became Elijah's disciple (1 Kgs. 19:19–21).
- *Battle reports* of significant military engagements, for example, the defeat of the Canaanite city of Ai (Jos. 7:2–5).
- *Construction accounts* of important buildings or objects where there is great attention to detail like the building of the Temple (1 Kgs. 6 – 7).
- *Special experiences* such as dreams, being met by an angel or encountering God can be retold in either the first or third person. *Dreams* are usually followed by an interpretation as when Joseph assisted his fellow prisoners in the Egyptian jail (Gen. 40:9–11; 16–17). *Epiphanies* normally report an experience in which God or the angel of the Lord appears with a special message. Moses' encounter at the burning bush is a good example of an epiphany (Ex. 3:2–12).
- *Historical reports* are rather more elaborate than ordinary reports. They can contain dialogue, dramatic touches and may even possess the development of a rudimentary plot. Saul's first reported acts as king in

---

[3] In what follows see William W. Klein et al, *Introduction to Biblical Interpretation*, 261–70.

rescuing the city of Jabesh would fall into this category
(1 Sam. 11:1–11).

- *Memoirs* are the experiences of an individual, written
  by them to illustrate the history of the era in which they
  lived. The accounts of the respective returns from exile
  to Jerusalem of Ezra and Nehemiah illustrate this well
  (Ezra 7:27 – 9:15; Neh. 1:1 – 7:73a).

2. *Heroic narratives* are common within the Old Testament
and consist of a number of episodes that concentrate on the
exploits of an individual who has risen to heroic status.
Moses, Joshua and the Judges are such heroes. Moses
brings the People of Israel out of Egypt, through the wilderness and to the brink of the Promised Land having received
God's law on the way (Exodus – Deuteronomy). Joshua
leads them on from there in conquest of the land, beginning
with Jericho (Jos. 1 – 6). In the first part of Genesis these
heroic narratives take on epic status. In literature, epics
address a society's formative influences and identity. The
narratives are therefore broad in scope and often are played
out against a supernatural backdrop. This is true in the
cycle of stories in Genesis 1 – 11.

Cosmic Epics recount the story of ultimate origins, not
only of a nation but of the whole cosmos. In the accounts of
Adam and Eve in the garden (1 – 3), Noah and the great
flood (6 – 9) and the story of the separation of the nations
(10 – 11) God is actively involved.

Ancestral Epics pick up nationalistic themes with the destiny of the heroes being inextricably linked to the future of
the nation. Genesis 12 – 36 consists of a series of ancestral
epics with the Patriarchal narratives of Abraham, Isaac,
Jacob and his sons. Israelite history flows from these narratives and her future destiny is defined by them. Indeed,
being 'a people of the promise' is a constant theme within

their national identity. The stories of Joshua and the rise of King David could also be viewed in this light.

3. Prophet Stories retell the life of a prophet and illustrate the God-honouring qualities of a life lived in communion with Yahweh. Elijah and Elisha exercise tenacity and persistence under pressure from those in political authority (1 Kgs. 17 – 2 Kgs. 9) while Daniel demonstrates fidelity to the faith in an alien culture with complete confidence in God's sovereignty (Dan. 1 – 6).

4. Comedy means something quite different in contemporary entertainment to what it does in the study of literature. While it may aim to amuse in places the defining factor is that it is a 'happy ever after story'. The book of Esther concludes happily with her triumph over the treachery of Haman. The story of Joseph is a comedy too, with a number of amusing reversals in the plot and the positive outcome for the family of Israel (Gen. 37 – 50).

5. The Gospels and Acts are familiar as they relate the stories of Jesus and the birth of the early church to us. They are not objective historical narratives in the modern sense as they have a clearly identified purpose in the mission and teaching of the Christian community. John is quite clear: 'These are written that you may believe that Jesus is the Christ, the Son of God, and that by believing you have life in his name' (Jn. 20:31). Luke commends his own two-volume work to an individual named Theophilus, 'that you may know the certainty of the things you have been taught' (Lk. 1:1–4; Acts 1:1).

6. Apocalypse can be found in the books of Daniel in the Old Testament and Revelation in the New Testament. It is quite unlike anything else. Indeed, on reading it you might be forgiven for thinking it was the script of a horror movie rather than an important religious text. The nearest contemporary genre we have to the bizarre images of this style of storytelling is the art of political cartoons. During the Cold War the picture of an eagle painted with gaudy stripes and stars, circling ominously over the head of a large bear branded with the mark of the hammer and sickle and reaching out to grasp the eagle would not have been unusual. Understanding the animals as the national symbols of the USA and USSR helps the reader understand the cartoonists humour. Similarly, understanding the images contained in Daniel and Revelation begins to unlock their secrets as they comment at one and the same time on both contemporary events and the end of history.

These six categories give an overview of the main kinds of narrative material to be found in the Bible. Together they act as a reminder of how pervasive stories are in the Scriptures. Conservative estimates identify narrative as comprising over two-thirds of the text.[4] This should be no surprise. The Christian experience of faith is rooted in 'telling the story'. In the evangelical tradition the emphasis of the story of salvation centres around the redemptive death of Jesus on the cross, the climax of God's reconciling intent for humankind. In the liturgical tradition the rhythm of the Christian year is paced by the festivals of Christmas, Easter and Pentecost. Each festival is centred on a landmark narrative from the New Testament, thus ensuring the story of decisive redemptive activity is annually retold to God's

---

[4] The actual percentage depends upon how various portions of the Bible are categorised. Carl Grasser calculated the narrative content of the Bible at 77 per cent in *Concordia Theology Monthly* while H. Grady Davis estimated it at 90 per cent in, *Design for Preaching*, 157.

people with suitable periods of expectation and preparation in Advent and Lent.

For years preachers have been schooled in the art of enabling us as believers to connect 'our stories with The Story'. This is what we do, whether by means of evangelical conversion experience, the seasonal expectation of the liturgical calendar, or indeed through both. The aim is to bring together the story of our lives with the ongoing story of salvation in Jesus Christ.

Here is another critical observation about 'our story'. At this moment in time each of us is actively and intimately involved in living out the story of our own lives. As Brian Wicker puts it, 'We dream in narrative, daydream in narrative, remember, anticipate, hope, despair, believe, doubt, plan, revise, criticize, construct, gossip, learn, hate, and love by narrative.'[5] Our lives are full of stories; they are of the essence of being alive. We may not share our 'life-story' with everyone we meet, but any conversation of any depth is littered with anecdotes, funny stories and mini-narratives from our life experience.

Some scholars have argued that experiencing our lives as narrative is fundamental to our existence and is a universal condition of human consciousness. The argument goes like this. We live in the present amid a temporal flow of actions and events. The only way we can connect to this ever-present temporal flow and bring unity to our experience is through developing an understanding of what is happening to us. This requires that we conceive of the past and develop a memory for what has happened, alongside imagining the future and anticipating what is to come. In this way, a simple understanding of the narrative structure of

---

[5] Brian Wicker, *The Story-Shaped World: Fiction and Metaphysics: Some Variations on a Theme*, in David L. Larsen, *Telling the Old, Old Story: The Art of Narrative Preaching*, 30.

our lives comes into being. Indeed, some have concluded that such a narrative understanding is foundational to human consciousness. They maintain that, no matter what a person's origin in time or culture, everyone tends to organise their experience in a narrative form. As a consequence, everyone discovers that stories fit with their experience of life.[6]

It seems, therefore, as though God has created us to live in a universe where narrative and stories define who we are. This is true for us in our individual experience. While I was in the United States in the mid-1990s I was asked to identify the key elements of my life story. I was shocked at how British I was in the company of American, Canadian and Korean colleagues. Indeed, it went much further than that. It was not only my musical tastes, favourite food and my allegiance to Norwich City Football Club that bore the thumb print of my personal story. My theology, my philosophy of life, my personal commitments and passions could all be explained by reference to some part of my life story which had proven to be a formative influence.

The psychologists have always told us that 'the child is father of the man'. As hackneyed and inappropriately gender specific as this one-liner is, it remains true. The narrative of our lives, the experiences we have and the choices we make define our personal identity. Yet it goes still further, beyond the immediacy of our own personal experience. The stories handed down through our families also help us to locate ourselves in the world. Some embrace their family heritage; others may choose to define their identity against

---

[6]   For a fuller discussion see Stephen Crites, 'The Narrative Quality of Experience', *Journal of the American Academy of Religion* 39 (September 1971) as cited by Richard L. Eslinger, *Narrative Imagination: Preaching the Worlds That Shape Us*, 5–12, and Stanley Hauerwas and L. Gregory Jones (eds.), *Why Narrative?: Readings in Narrative Theology*, 66ff.

their family background so that their present life bears little resemblance to where they have come from. Either way, their family story has exerted a strong influence over them, whether this story is viewed in a positive or negative light. Maybe this is part of the explanation why those without knowledge of their family tree can become consumed by the need to discover their past. Not to have such an anchor is to feel rootless and cast adrift.

Outside of family background our denominational, national and other identities are forged through the stories that are common to us. I was brought up as a Methodist and ministered first as an evangelist and then as a Pastor within the Methodist denomination. I have a lifelong love of John Wesley; I adore Charles Wesley's hymns and am thoroughly Arminian in my theology. Having become a Baptist Minister nothing properly prepared me for moving to another denomination where the 'family stories' were different and looking far more towards the Reformation than the evangelical revival. In reality the denominations are very similar as both are part of British Nonconformity. However, I have had to conclude that I will forever be a strange denominational hybrid.

National identity is very similar. When I was studying in the United States I was amused by the aptness of Churchill's statement that America and Britain are two countries separated by the same language. The common use of English gives a superficial appearance of similarity. However, the stories by which we define our respective national identities are often in conflict. For example, in the UK the churches have long benefited from the establishment of the Church of England as the state-sanctioned religion. This has ring-fenced a daily act of worship in state schools and the presence of Bishops in the legislative process as members of the House of Lords. In the USA the separation of church and state is a fundamental tenet of the constitution and is constantly policed by groups like the American Civil Liberties Union. When I first spent time in the United States it was a disorientating experience to be in a country that was so familiar through various shared cultural landmarks and yet be so clearly an alien. Long tracts of the history that I had grown up with and many of the stories that helped to define who I was were not shared by those with whom I studied.

This is the world that God has created for us to live in. It should really be no surprise that the Scriptures are so loaded with narrative. 'It begins with the tale of a garden, and ends with the city of gold.' There is purpose and direction in the biblical narrative. We have a past which proclaims that God created this world for us, saw that it was good and blessed it. Scripture is then the history of God's interaction with this world. It has to do with his working out his purposes in our realm of existence. His purposes culminated in the life, death and resurrection of Jesus Christ. Now, post-Pentecost, we live as believers in the outworking of these events. Our eyes are fixed firmly on the future and the end of history as we know it. 'Amen. Come Lord Jesus' (Rev. 22:20).

The Bible is a timeline that runs from the Garden of Eden to the City of Gold. As Robert Alter has said, the basic theological quest of the biblical writers is, 'to reveal the enactments of God's purpose in history'.[7] They saw history as having a shape that is rooted in the control of divine purpose.

The narratives of the Bible are not merely a literary technique or device being used by the writers to accomplish their ends. Narrative and storytelling are altogether more important than that. Through this literary form the biblical narratives actually embody how things are. God has given

---

[7] Robert Alter, *The Art of Biblical Narrative*, 33.

us a book full of stories because he has created us to live within a narrative-defined experience of history. For Thomas Long,

> The correspondence between the narrative form and the biblical writer's basic perception of reality may also tell us why there is no biblical term for 'story'. In the Bible, narrative is not a device; it is an expression of the way things are.[8]

Simply put, narrative is integral to the structure of reality that God has created. If this is such a crucial part of how God has created both our understanding of reality and the way we communicate together, we ought to pay it careful attention as preachers of the gospel.

---

[8] Thomas G. Long, *Preaching and the Literary Forms of the Bible*, 69.

3

How Does Narrative Work?

Narratives are everywhere. Like the air we breathe they are all around us. Most obviously in novels, films and TV programmes they range from thriller series to soap operas, comedies, news reports and advertisements. Narratives also inhabit the full range of human experience from our historic myths and legends, through conversational anecdotes to our own personal histories with their dreams and nightmares. Some have argued that narrative is so widespread that it must be one of the 'deep structures' of our makeup, somehow genetically 'hard-wired' into our minds.[1] Certainly the early indicators of narrative ability begin to appear in children in their third or fourth year. You only have to witness their sheer delight at having a story read to them or their appetite to watch and re-watch a favourite film or TV programme to appreciate that narrative is fundamental to our human makeup. Indeed, without the ability to construct and understand stories it would be very difficult to order and communicate our experience of time.

In 1966 the influential scholar Roland Barthes wrote a highly significant essay in which he observed that narrative was:

---

[1] H. Porter Abbott, *The Cambridge Introduction to Narrative*, 3.

present in every age, in every place, in every society; it begins with the very history of mankind and there nowhere is nor has been a people without narrative. All classes, all human groups, have their narratives ... narrative is international, transhistorical, transcultural: it is simply there, like life itself. [2]

While narrative may have been an essential part of the human condition from the beginning, the twentieth century gave birth to an era of mass storytelling with the advent of radio, cinema, TV, the internet and the explosion of print media. Journalist Robert Fulford characterises this phenomenon as the growth of industrialised narrative – storytelling that is designed for mass reproduction, distribution and consumption. Going hand in hand with this high density of narrative in everyday life is the growth of leisure and the opportunity to absorb these different narratives as entertainment. [3]

So, what is a narrative? A basic definition would be to see it as a representation of an event or series of events. To say, 'I have a five year old son' is a description. It is not a narrative because there is no action, there are no events. However, to relate that, 'I took my son to school this morning' may not be a compelling story to listen to, but it is a narrative in its most basic form. Of course, there are many stories that are not told. Narrative takes shape when events are told from one person to another. Therefore it is important to recognise that it always includes three components, a tale, a teller and an addressee. [4]

---

[2] Roland Barthes, 'Introduction to the Structural Analysis of Narratives', in Susan Sontag (ed.), *A Barthes Reader*, 251–2.

[3] Robert Fulford, *The Triumph of Narrative: Storytelling in the Age of Mass Media*, 149–50.

[4] Abbott, *Narrative*, 12 and Michael Toolan, *Narrative: A Critical Linguistic Introduction*, 1–2. NB, throughout this chapter I will use the terms addressee, narratee, listener, viewer, reader and audience interchangeably as sits best in the context. In each case, they identify those for whom a narrative is produced.

Looking at the history of narrative many scholars identify Homer, the Greek poet and author of the two long
narrative poems *The Iliad* and *The Odyssey*, as the ultimate
ancestor of the European novel and the Western narrative
tradition. However, this storytelling tradition has a further
foundation in the books of the Bible. These biblical stories,
especially those from the Old Testament, have been influential in many ways, putting an emphasis on characters as well
as events, and an 'explanatory mode' that seeks to reflect on
the story for its relative significance and the moral values
that might be derived from its events.[5]

The power of storytelling is in the way that the unfolding plot of a story mimics our own experience of life and
the way reality unfolds sequentially for us as people. As
such, narrative produces the feeling of events happening in
time and evokes a personal and often emotional response
from those listening to it. Whether true or false in what it
depicts, it appears to replicate life. This is the reason for its
penetration of our collective imagination and its dominance as a means of communication over against more
analytical approaches. For Fulford this is 'the triumph of
narrative'.[6]

The increasing appreciation of the importance of narrative in contemporary communication led to the latter part
of the twentieth century witnessing a rapid growth of
research and writing on the subject. Narrative theory, or
'narratology', attempts to explore the central questions
concerning our use of storytelling and how its various

---

[4] (*Continued*) will use the terms addressee, narratee, listener,
viewer, reader and audience interchangeably as sits best in the
context. In each case, they identify those for whom a narrative is
produced.

[5] Paul Cobley, *Narrative*, 41–51.

[6] Fulford, *Triumph*, 15–16.

parts work together to produce a dynamic means of communication.[7] What follows in this chapter is an overview of some of the basic components of narrative which it would be helpful for a preacher exploring a narrative style to be aware of.[8]

Turning a Story into a Narrative

In everyday speech the tendency is to use the words story and narrative interchangeably, with story clearly being the more popular term. However, with those who have thought more systematically about the subject a clear distinction in definition is made to identify different stages in the process of retelling events:

- *Story* – is the chronological series of events that happened as experienced by identified individuals, i.e. a summary of what actually happened.
- *Narrative* – is the sum total of devices and procedures that are used to shape and develop the story into a finished work. These include various strategies like plot development and characterisation. It may not follow a strict chronological sequence and can also be

---

[7] Jakob Lothe, *Narrative in Fiction and Film: An Introduction*, vii. Lothe defines narrative theory as, 'a tool for analysis and interpretation – a necessary aid to a better understanding of narrative texts through close reading'. 9.

[8] A fuller exploration of narrative theory which includes the general critical theories that have been employed in narrative analysis in recent study, such as Russian Formalism, the Chicago School, structuralism, archetypal criticism and deconstruction, can be found in Brian Richardson (ed.), *Narrative Dynamics: Essays on Plot, Time, Closure, and Frames*.

selective by passing over some things while concentrating on others.[9]

In understanding story and narrative in this way, story always seems to pre-exist narrative, and narrative itself is always a re-presentation of an existing story.

There are a number of fundamental ingredients to a story/narrative that have been identified:

- *Events* – are, simply put, what happened. Some might call them the actions of a story.
- *Characters* – designate who the events happened to. Indeed, very often the events are completely caught up with, and even controlled by, the actions and reactions of the characters involved. Sometimes, however, characters are defined as entities. When the main subject of a story is not human (an animal or an alien), or is even inanimate, character may not be the best designation. For example, 'The volcano erupted and destroyed all the surrounding forest and vegetation', is an embryonic narrative with no characters present at all.
- *Setting* – while a common feature of story/narrative, it is not essential. 'I fell down' is a simple story without a setting. However, where simple stories are elaborated, setting is very likely to emerge.
- *A crisis-resolution progression* – again, while this is a common feature of story/narrative, it is not essential either. Yet it is recognised as the core element in the

---

[9] In narrative theory the designations of story and narrative roughly correspond to the categories of *fabula/syuzhet* of the Russian formalists and *histoire/discourse* in the more recent French work of Barthes et al. cf. Lothe, *Fiction and Film*, 7; Richardson (ed.), *Narrative Dynamics*, 130–1; Toolan, *Narrative*, 10–11.

development of a plot and, arguably, is the most significant component of making a narrative enjoyable to those who listen.

Seeking to more closely define the nature of narrative, Michael Toolan identifies six typical characteristics that can be observed.[10] They are:

1. *A degree of artificial fabrication or constructedness* – the narrative has been worked upon and its sequence, emphasis and pace are usually carefully planned.
2. *An element of prefabrication* – in that certain parts of the narrative seem familiar from elsewhere, having been imported into the text. For example, we know that the character in the role of the hero will save the day.
3. *A trajectory* – narratives are usually going somewhere. Aristotle, in his *Poetics*, stipulated that they should have beginnings, middles and endings.
4. *A narrator* – someone has to be 'telling the story'. They may be an identifiable individual who is part of the story or they may be an anonymous background figure, but it is through their eyes that the story is retold.
5. *A tendency to exploit spatio-temporal displacement* – that ability of language to refer to things or events that are removed or distant in time or space from either the speaker or the addressee.
6. *An ability to recall happenings remote from the teller or their audience.* This is about memory, a uniquely human ability. Narrative is about reliving our memories.

When looking at how a narrative is conveyed it is significant to take note of the process involved. Some have identified

---

[10] Toolan, *Narrative*, 4–6.

this as a 'Model of Narrative Communication'.[11] Clearly, in a book based narrative, there is a movement from the origin of a text, through its written form, to the reader. This is simply illustrated in Fig. 1 below.

Figure 1 *A Model of Narrative Communication*

Real Author →
  Implied Author →
    Narrator →
      Narratee →
        Implied Reader →
          Real Reader

In this model the perspective is nuanced slightly differently at each stage. To avoid unnecessary misconceptions and to properly understand and interpret the text of a narrative, these different structural elements need to be clearly identified.

The three most obvious positions in the model are those of the *real author*, the *narrator* and the *real reader*. The real author wrote the text, the narrator is the voice that narrates the events and the real reader is the person who picks up the book to read. A common misunderstanding is to always see the narrator as representative of the voice of the historical author. While this may be so, it is not necessarily the case at all. The narrator may themselves be a fictional character with a perspective quite different from the historical author.

The *implied author* is the picture of the writer that the reader assembles on the basis of what they have read and seen of the image of the author in the text. It may be quite different from the author themselves. The *implied reader* is who we perceive to be the intended recipient of the narrative. At a basic level the implied reader of a children's book is a child, but the real reader may be their parent.

---

[11] Lothe, *Fiction and Film*, 13–21.

The Narratee is the person who is directly addressed by the narrator. In Charlotte Bronte's, *Jane Eyre*, the narratee is disclosed as the real reader when the narrator exclaims, 'Reader, I married him.'[12] By contrast the narratee of the Gospel of Luke and the Acts of the Apostles is an unknown individual named Theophilus (Lk. 1:3; Acts 1:1).

Finding the Plot: The Narrative Road Map

We say that someone has 'lost the plot' when their actions don't correspond to their perceived intentions. Simply put, a plot is the way events and characters are organised in a narrative to induce curiosity and suspense. Yet it is much more than that. Plot is the mechanism by which the events of a story are combined, structured and developed to become a compelling account that grips the attention of a listener. Plot is the shaping force of every narrative discourse[13] and is the means by which it moves forward.

It has already been noted above that Aristotle believed that a narrative should have a beginning, middle and an end; however these are only some of his best-known observations about how plots[14] developed. He also maintained that the beginnings and endings should not be arbitrary in any way; rather they were to be crafted and intentional. The narratives themselves should be of a certain magnitude, organic in unity and complete in themselves. Preferring a single plot, rather than a multi-layered creation with numerous sub-plots, he saw that events should be connected by probable and necessary progression and should

---

[12] Charlotte Bronte, *Jane Eyre*, 379.
[13] Peter Brooks, *Reading for the Plot: Design and Intention in Narrative*, 13.
[14] Or, as he termed them, 'mythos'.

avoid irrelevant incidents and a descent into a more epi-
sodic form.[15]

Of the beginnings of a narrative Aristotle said, 'a beginning
is that which does not itself follow anything by causal necessity, but after which something naturally is or comes to be'.

On the subject of endings he acknowledges how difficult
they are to properly achieve the required closure, 'many tie
the knot well but unravel it ill'. He disapproves of happy
endings for evil protagonists and painful ones for virtuous
ones. His preference is for tragedy in which emotions of pity
and fear are brought to resolution in a cathorsis of the
emotions. Yet he recognises that many authors sidestep it in
order to play to the weakness of the audience.[16]

Historically it is the subject of the plot that has been the
most discussed and debated among those who study narrative. From Aristotle to the twentieth century, most writers
and critics alike have favoured a plausible, unified, causally
connected plot form. The experiments of some more contemporary writers with a virtually plotless approach have
never really taken off. Modern audiences seem to require
more complex motivations, sub-plots and resolutions with
a multi-layered approach typified by Tolkien's *Lord of the
Rings* trilogy. The popularity of Tolkien's work in both its
literary form – celebrated by the BBC as the best-loved book
in the UK – and the widely acclaimed movie adaptation
by Peter Jackson highlight the overwhelming power of a
brilliantly conceived and imaginative plot.

Central to the development of a plot are the exper-
ientially engaging effects of suspense and surprise.
Frequently, these occur at the very beginning of a narrative
as well as being peppered throughout the rest of the plot
in strategic places. Illustrative of this principle are the obser-

---

[15] Richardson, *Narrative Dynamics*, 64.
[16] Richardson, *Narrative Dynamics*, 249–50; Abbot, *Narrative*,
163.

vations of the Russian narratologist, Vladimir Propp, who noted that in the overarching structure of the Russian fairytale an initial state of equilibrium was disturbed by various turbulent forces. The turbulence brings disequilibrium and upheaval before the action of the narrative restores the equilibrium by returning things to how they should be, albeit in a modified way.

A simple plot might be seen as moving through four stages or transitions:

1. *Exposition* – the part of the story that sets the scene, introduces characters and sets up the initial turbulence and consequent disequilibrium.
2. *Complication* – where the story and the characters within it find that things move from bad to worse.
3. *Climax* – suspense is at its highest, the outcome is not clear and matters are most threatening.
4. *Resolution* – a solution to the problems is introduced and denouement follows. Though the ending does not have to be a happy one.[17]

For British writer, E.M. Forster, the difference between a story and a plot was that for the first we say, 'and then' as it is a narrative of events arranged in their own time sequence. For a plot we ask, 'why?' For Forster, a plot is not typified by the mere curiosity evoked by wanting to know what happens next, but rather by the intelligence and memory required to fathom out the 'why?' question. Story is merely factual and can be mentally picked up by simply running the eye across a page. By contrast, a highly organised novel does not so easily reveal its content. Understanding comes by relating one set of information with another and wrestling

---

[17] Peter Abbs and John Richardson, *The Forms of Narrative: A Practical Guide*, 107.

with the mystery that sits at the centre of any plot. In this way, it can be observed that narrative is an intelligent medium. More than this, it also requires the related quality of memory. The plot-maker expects the listener to remember. Words and actions matter and should be constantly mulled over and cross-related to discover new clues and new chains of cause and effect.[18]

The Narrator: Who Sees? Who Tells?

Whether it is a novel, a film, a biography or a radio drama, no narrative that we listen to is a pure recounting of what happened. All narrative is mediated. The question is, by whom? Who sees what happens? Who tells the story? This is a significant choice on the part of the author. The narrator of the story is a very influential figure. Whether they are a clearly identifiable character or someone who sits more anonymously in the background, the narrator influences the readers understanding and can colour it with their own bias. Michael Toolan sees the bid to be a narrator in many life situations as a bid for power. Whether the narrator is a journalist, a politician, or an employer conducting a performance appraisal, the person who tells the story is the person who is in the position of influence and control. Narrators, by virtue of their role, are ordinarily granted a level of trust and authority as a matter of course because this is a fundamental convention of narrative. However, this position of trust can be abused and exploited and gives rise to what scholars identify as 'unreliable narration'. Such misrepresentation is painfully difficult to unravel. Take, for example, the judges summing up in a fraud case where a

---

[18] E.M. Forster, 'Story and Plot', in Richardson, *Narrative Dynamics*, 71–2.

defendant who pleaded innocent is found guilty. Toolan observes: 'the sentencing judge often refers to the obfuscating detailed deception that has been uncovered as "a complex tissue of systematic distortion and fabrication", or uses a similar revealing description'.[19]

Recognising the significant position of influence that a narrator has alongside the trust and authority that is invested in the role, the questions for an author to decide is, who sees the action and who tells the story? Whose voice do we hear giving the narration? The basic identification is a grammatical one, that of 'person'. There are two principal designations, first person ('I went to church this morning and arrived late') and third person ('She went to church this morning and arrived late'). There have been some experiments with second-person narrative ('You went to church this morning and arrived late'), but this has never been particularly popular, probably because we do not appreciate being addressed in this manner.

By their very nature, a first-person narrator is taken up in the plot itself. Whether a major or minor character, their knowledge of what is happening and their engagement with events is determined by the plausibility of their character and their place in the unfolding drama. It is a powerful genre as it is laced with firsthand experience of the action and its impact upon them physically and psychologically.

The third-person narrator is very different. They do not participate in the events that are retold and rather sit outside or 'above' the plot. Their motivation in presenting the narrative is less immediate and personal, but this is balanced by a much wider understanding of event and the psychology of the characters as their role is more omniscient and God-like. The third-person narrative is the oldest and most common method of telling a story.

---

[19] Toolan, *Narrative*, 3.

As was indicated above, it is important to remember that the author and the narrator are not necessarily the same person. This is especially true in novels and other narratives that flow from the creative arts. The narrator is just as much an integral part of the narrative as the characters in the story. The narrator is a creation of the author as a means to present and develop their text. Indeed, even the narrative voice of journalists may not be their own personal view but, rather, that of the editorial stance of their organisation.

It is important to continue to recognise this as every story is always charged with meaning. Having worked extensively in journalism, Robert Fulford, a Canadian, is adamant that, 'There is no such thing as just a story.'[20] He contends that it is impossible to have a value free narrative as the very reason narratives are told and retold is because they have meaning. A story survives and is remembered because it has earned the right to, it means something. Good narratives connect with our deeply held principles and values while calling forth ethical judgements from those who listen to them.

While narrative theorists would rather talk about 'focalisation', 'orientation' or 'narrative perspective' than the vaguer and more disputed term 'point of view', there is no doubt that it is almost inevitable that such a position is adopted as events are retold. In its simplest form, the fairy tale beginning, 'Once upon a time in a distant land there lived a beautiful princess' automatically signals through the words 'Once', 'distant' and the past tense 'lived' that there is a contrast between the remoteness in space and time of the narrative when compared with the proximity of the teller-listener.

---

[20] Fulford, *Triumph*, 6.

The perspective of a narrative does not have to remain static either. The longer the story and the more sophisticated the plot the greater the variation can be. Douglas Coupland's, *Hey Nostradamus*, effects this variation in perspective openly with different sections of the book being written in the first person by different characters. Other strategies are more subtle. However, the perspectives of different characters that Coupland uses are a helpful example which demonstrates that it is not only perspectives of space and time that are involved. How we think, what we feel and what we believe are also involved.[21]

The questions 'who sees' and 'who tells' are therefore vitally important for properly understanding the narrative and its perspective.

The Setting: When and Where?

The concept of 'space-time' was introduced to the world through Einstein's Theory of Relativity and is much loved by followers of *Star Trek* and other sci-fi books and movies. Time is the fourth dimension of space and the two are inseparably linked. Time and space are also intrinsically connected in narrative. When and where did these events happen? These are questions of setting and context.

It is not essential to have a setting for a narrative to work. Yet, as people, we have a strong desire to establish an identifiable context in which the events of a story take place.[22] The setting itself can have a significant influence on the narrative; indeed, it can either cause or affect how characters are and behave. In *The Matrix* trilogy of films the

---

[21] What Rimmon-Kenan identifies as the major facets of focalisation, the perceptual, the psychological and the ideological. Cf. Toolan, *Narrative*, 59–63 and Lothe, *Fiction and Film*, 38–45.
[22] Abbott, *Narrative*, 17 and Toolan, *Narrative*, 91.

awakening of Neo to his context of life in a virtual reality is
determinative for the whole plot of the series. Interacting
with the timing of an Olympic heat on the Sabbath introduces a significant plot complication in the movie *Chariots
of Fire* for Eric Liddell, one of the leading characters.
Indeed, some would go so far as to maintain that characters
in a narrative are created by their context.[23]

Setting is often used to trigger accepted stereotypes of
understanding in an audience. This can be undertaken with
diametrically opposite objectives. Sometimes an author will
use a stereotype to communicate quickly with their audience about the nature of the context or the characters
within it, drawing on the pre-existing experience of the listeners. Jesus does this with the parable of The Prodigal Son
(Lk. 15:11–32). Other times stereotyping will be deployed
to add a diversion to the plot, only to explode the stereotype
at a later stage and powerfully drive home a particular point
having drawn the audience into the deception. Jesus' parable of The Good Samaritan is a telling example of such a
strategy (Lk. 10:25–37). Notice in both of these examples
how the sense of 'place' is to a great degree defined by the
nature of the characters present.

The setting in which a narrative is framed also affects its
meaning and reception. As Ross Chambers states:

> consider, for example, a 'faggot' joke told by gay people
> among themselves, by straight people among themselves,
> [and] by a straight person to a gay person ... In each of these
> cases, the significance of the story is determined less by its ac-
> tual content than by the point of its being told, that is, the rela-
> tionships mediated by the act of narration.[24]

---

[23] Noah Lukeman, *The Plot Thickens*, 171.
[24] Richardson (ed.), *Narrative Dynamics*, 2–3.

If it is important to understand how characters relate to and interact with their setting, narrative theory has also found it helpful to identify how a narrator also relates to the narrative context. One of the concepts that has been beneficial in this regard is that of 'distance'. It relates particularly to the relationship between the narrator and the events/characters in the narrative text. Jakob Lothe finds it helpful to see this by means of a three-way division of the concept:[25]

1. *Temporal distance* – As narrative normally involves a process of looking back in retrospect, this indicates the difference in time between the narrator and the events that are narrated.
2. *Spatial distance* – This refers to the physical location of the events in contrast to the context of the narrator.
3. *Attitudinal distance* – This is the level of insight the narrator has into the characters in the text and the judgements and values that are made over of the events that occur in the narrative.

When examining the role that time plays in any given narrative and the issues it raises, the insights of Gérard Genette and his threefold analysis have been widely adopted.[26]

1. *Order* – that is, the sequence of the narrated events. Does the narrative simply assume the chronological pattern of the actual story or not? Most narrative does not begin at the beginning or end at the end. Rather, through use of flashback and foreshadowing, a more complex and intriguing pattern of moving through time is created.

---

[25] Lothe, *Fiction and Film*, 34–6.
[26] Gérard Genette, 'Order, Duration, and Frequency', in Richardson (ed.), *Narrative Dynamics*, 25–34.

2. *Duration* – the relationship between the extent of time that the events are supposed to cover and the proportion of the narrative that is actually used to present them. This produces the pace of a text. Acceleration of pace can indicate that a particular time frame in the narrative is less important and is therefore being passed over, while a deceleration is frequently taken as a marker by the author that what follows is significant. Genette illustrates his observation by reference to Marcel Proust's *A la recherche du temps perdu*, where he charts the extremes present in the text where a decade is summarised by one sentence and two to three hours is covered by 190-pages. In sections of the book the pace shifts from one page per century to one page per minute.

3. *Frequency* – relates to how often something happens in the story compared with how often it is narrated in the text. For example, the Apostle Paul's conversion on the road to Damascus happened only once, but the story is retold by Luke in the Acts of the Apostles no fewer than three times (Acts 9:1–19; 22:3–16; 26:9–18). Alternatively, an event that was a multiple occurrence can be summarised in the narrative by a single reference. Luke relates of Jesus that, 'on the Sabbath day he went into the synagogue, as was his custom' (Lk. 4:16). Frequency in this sense is not to be confused with other strategies an author may use to accomplish different purposes. This can include such things as the repetition of a certain mannerism to help develop a character's place in the text or the regular restatement of an underlying theme or motif that lies behind their reason for writing the narrative.

Characterisation: Creating People

Aristotle believed that action in a plot was far more important than characters. A character's main contribution to a
narrative was primarily as a performer of actions, to which
they were subordinate in significance. By the end of the
nineteenth century, for men like Leslie Stephen,[27] the exact
opposite was true. The great object of narrative action was
the revelation of character. A middle way is perhaps most
acceptable. The logic is undeniable that event and action
involve people, and that their outcome is determined by the
nature of the people involved. Likewise, the experience of
the action in a narrative has a forming as well as a revealing
role on the characters caught up in it.

There can be no doubt that insights into the minds and
character of imagined others, their uniqueness of motive
and difference of worldview, is powerfully attractive to the
contemporary reader. At one level it is a kind of voyeurism,
at another it is a journey into self-awareness. Yet characterisation is an illusion into which the author must draw the
reader as an accomplice, drawing on personal experience
and filling in the gaps to properly visualise the imaginary
person. Narrative characters are then, at least in part, mod-
elled on a reader's own conception of people.[28]

Some theorists maintain that any narrative character is
based upon a double illusion. The first illusion is that the
person does not really exist and is therefore nothing more
than a verbal fabrication. The second illusion involves the
presumption that reading the external signs from a narrative character gives corresponding insight into their
supposed hidden inner nature. Real life teaches us that this

---

[27] Leslie Stephen was appointed first editor of the *Dictionary of National Biography* in 1881.
[28] Toolan, *Narrative*, 80–1.

is not necessarily so. Yet the power of narrative is demonstrated as it irresistibly invites us to construct mental images of characters that are illusory.[29]

E.M. Forster introduced the concepts of 'flat' and 'round' narrative characters in the late 1920s with his, *Aspects of the Novel*. Flat characters have no complexity and depth and are, therefore, flat. Round characters, by contrast, have varying degrees of depth and complexity and, in Forster's words, 'cannot be summed up in a single phrase'.[30] Indeed, characters become more believable as they develop and become more complex and multidimensional. Heroes can be flawed, and individuals can act in paradoxical and sometimes self-contradictory ways.

Characterisation can be accomplished by an author either directly or indirectly. Direct definition is achieved by the author through direct summary using adjectives and abstract nouns. The persuasive power of this approach is not uniform, but it is best realised with an authoritative or omniscient narrator.

Indirect characterisation is demonstrated, dramatised or exemplified by the character in the narrative itself. Action, speech, external appearance and behaviour are the normal means by which such insights are communicated by the author. Sometimes, too, the author will use the setting to heighten some perceived quality in the make-up of a character. So, a cowboy riding unhurriedly in the open country of the Wild West relays something of his freedom and carefree attitude to life.

Noah Lukeman, advising authors as to how they might bring their narratives to life, counsels them to fully chart the facts of their character's life and the depths of their psyche before they begin to write. He then explores over forty

---

[29] Lothe, *Fiction and Film*, 78.
[30] E.M. Forster, *Aspects of the Novel*, 69.

categories of the external and inner life as the way to begin to do that. These include:

Physical appearance	Motivations
Clothes and grooming	Values and vices
Medical background	Politics and ideology
Family background	Relationship to food
Employment	Friendships
Education	Habits
Residence	Hobbies
Romantic history	Sexual preferences
Religion and spirituality	Level of self-awareness

Narrative Dynamics: Keeping the Story Moving

'Narrative dynamics' is the term that is used to refer to the way a narrative moves from its opening to its ending. It is an all-embracing term that covers the content of the narrative as well as its structure.[31] Authors produce movement by generating, sustaining, developing and then resolving the readers' interest in the narrative by a number of different means. This is accomplished by producing tension through exploiting instabilities that are either internal to the text or that potentially exist between the author and their audience. Within the text this means looking for instabilities that are created between various characters or through situations that may develop. These may then be further complicated and resolved through the telling of the narrative. Instabilities between the author and their audience

---

[31] Richardson (ed.), *Narrative Dynamics*, 2.

have their root in issues of value, belief, opinion, knowledge or expectation.

E.R. Braithwaite's novel, *To Sir With Love*, charts the difficulty of a new teacher establishing himself at an East End school in London following World War II. Internal narrative tension is created in a face-off between the raw teacher, learning his craft, and a group of articulate, unengaged pupils in their final months of formal education. Will he get through to them or not? The fact that he is black is a further plot complication in the developing narrative. However, external to the text the teacher's race raises significant cultural issues of belief and conviction for the audience with the story set in a neighbourhood of quintessentially traditional, white, working-class values. That the teacher, Rick Braithwaite, also has a white wife further complicates the potential instability between the author and his audience, as does the fact that Rick had become used to respect and gratitude for his service of King and country during the war while wearing his RAF uniform. A respect now universally absent in his experience.

Producing conflict is probably the most effective way to create tension for an audience. Boris Tomashevsky observed:

> The development of a story may generally be understood as a progress from one situation to another, so that each situation is characterized by a *conflict* of interest, by discord and struggle among the characters.[32]

The more complicated the conflict within a situation and the stronger the opposing interests of the characters, the greater the tension of the situation. Interestingly, at the bottom of the vast majority of conflicts the issue at stake is an issue of power, and who has it.

---

[32] Boris Tomashevsky, 'Story, Plot, and Motivation', in Richardson (ed.), *Narrative Dynamics*, 168.

The complimentary tool to conflict at the author's disposal is suspense. An audience looks for closure; indeed, they expect it, but not too soon. There is a sense in which an audience seems to tangibly enjoy the imbalance that precedes the closure. Skilled authors understand this and work hard to frustrate and then satisfy this desire to resolve the tension, deal with the conflict, and bring on the denouement. Yet it is a delicate balance that needs to be carefully nurtured. If the narrative is conducted at a continual peak of tension through conflict and suspense, ultimately the audience will get weary and begin to take the suspense less and less seriously.

The Audience: Keeping the Author's Target in View

My five-year-old son is a sophisticated consumer of narrative. At bedtime or in front of the TV he knows what he likes. It's interesting to watch which stories he comes back to time and again. By contrast, he doesn't get to the end of some stories. 'I don't like this!' he says, or, 'Can I go and do something else!' There is no hiding from his assessment.

Narrative is audience focused. Whether the objective is to merely entertain or to say something more important by communicating some loftier ideal through the medium, if you lose your audience, you've lost the plot. Lukeman suggests that an author's objective could be viewed as taking the audience through four stages with a narrative:[33]

1. *Curiosity* – this is the beginning. A listener is engaging with the narrative and wants to know more. They are prepared to listen and invest time, thought and attention into what the author has created. These are

---

[33] Lukeman, *Plot*, 199–201.

valuable commodities and need to be watched over wisely.

2. *Interest* – **by this point people are intrigued by the characters** and plot. Not everyone reaches this point, but they are not about to put the book down or start channel hopping on the TV. If someone else tried to change the channel they would be annoyed, but they are not hooked enough to need to see it through to the end yet.

3. *Need* – few works reach this stage. The viewer has become so transfixed by the characters and the plot that they '*need*' to know how things work out. Immersed in the narrative all sense of real time is lost. If it is a book that is being read it is likely that the person will stay up much later than the normal time they go to bed. They have to know what happened. With a TV soap or drama series it becomes a personal priority to see the next episode. You only have to examine the TV viewing ratings to see the correspondence between a plot climax and the number of people who tune in. If a plot cliff-hanger is left from the end of one series until the beginning of the next, it can be unbearable. 'Who shot JR?' was the question on the lips of *Dallas* fans around the world for the entire summer of 1980. Aware of the impact that the eventual revelation would acquire, the producers filmed several alternatives so that even the actors themselves did not know the answer. When, on 21 November, Kristin Shepard, pregnant with JR's child, was revealed as the would-be murderess, 80 per cent of American's watching TV that night were watching *Dallas*, making it the highest rated show in television history to that date.

4. *Action/Response* – this is the highest level of reaction that an author can expect to receive and a small number of works reach this level. Here, coming to the end of the narrative, putting the book down or leaving the

theatre is not enough. Change is in the air. There is a burning desire to do something in response. This may result in a change of attitudes and behaviour or it may lead to more direct action taken on the basis of what has been read or seen. Stephen Spielberg's movies *Amistad*, *Schindler's List* and *Saving Private Ryan* each had a measure of attitude changing response as audiences went home from movie theatres in hushed tones having been profoundly moved by what they had witnessed. John's Gospel was also written with the express intention of engaging the reader to change their beliefs and lifestyle as a consequence of having read the narrative it contained:

Jesus did many other miraculous signs in the presence of his disciples, which are not recorded in this book. But these are written that you may believe that Jesus is the Christ, the Son of God, and that by believing you may have life in his name (Jn. 20:30–31).

Part 2

Preaching in a Narrative Style

4

Finding The Plot

I remember one Sunday morning some years ago when we had a visiting preacher come to our church. He preached for over an hour and the congregation hung on his every word. He was a great storyteller and his sermon was powerfully laced with anecdotes that perfectly illustrated the points he was seeking to make from the Scriptures. Everyone was sitting glued to their seats as they listened, captivated, well past the time we normally concluded our services. Even those sections of our community that usually complained when the preacher 'went on a bit' were silenced and in awe. Years later, some of the stories he told remain fresh in my mind. Yet, as effective as this preaching event was with its liberal use of mini-narratives, it was not preaching in a narrative style.

It is easy to mistakenly believe that narrative style preaching is merely about increasing the number of stories we tell. It is not. Neither is it about strategically deploying biblical drama sketches, the dramatic reading of the Scriptures or one of the variety of approaches to storytelling that have become increasingly popular, especially among those exploring Celtic expressions of spirituality.

Preaching in a narrative style is a whole new way of thinking about how we engage with the practice of preaching. While a superficial appraisal might dismiss it as merely a change in style and structure, it is altogether more radical than that for those of us who have been schooled in a more traditional understanding of preaching.

At its heart, narrative style preaching is about the Christian community relearning and applying the insights of storytelling and the significance of narrative plot in our proclamation of the gospel. It centres on the structure and form of a sermon, yet much more is implied. It is far more of a fundamental shift in how we communicate than it first appears. Richard Jensen sees this shift as moving away from thinking and preaching in 'ideas' to thinking and preaching in 'story'. For him it is the inevitable consequence of the explosion in electronic communication and the birth of the post-literate age.[1] Adopting this style in preaching has a number of advantages. As we have already seen it is in harmony with the present cultural context as well as being thoroughly biblical. In addition, it also changes the manner in which we engage our listeners and help them learn.

Traditional preaching strategies are more deductive in style as the preacher shares with a congregation the fruit of their own research and prayerful reflection. A while ago I was preaching at the induction service of a minister who had just moved to a new church. The Bible passage we were looking at was Ephesians 4:1–16 which reaches a climax with Paul's statement, 'It was he who gave some to be apostles, some to be prophets, some to be evangelists, and some to be pastors and teachers'. In addressing the congregation, I identified three themes from the passage that were relevant to the beginning of a new ministry: namely, unity, growth and fitness. In the manner in which I had been taught, I told people we were looking at three themes from the passage, I explored them and then concluded with a summary and final illustration.

---

[1] Jensen, *Thinking in Story*, 8–9.

By contrast, the narrative style works far more inductively. The preacher seeks to take the members of a congregation on a journey of discovery. While the destination will have been clearly identified in the preacher's mind at the outset, to a greater or lesser degree individuals are left to make their own connections. A narrative passage of the Bible may confront the listener with the dilemmas faced by a character in the story, like when Paul arrived at Troas not sure where God was leading him next, or when Mary was faced with the inevitable conclusions of her local community following the discovery of her pregnancy. Some listeners get the point, others do not. Critics of the approach see this as a significant danger because of the loss of explicit biblical teaching. However, when someone makes a connection for themselves it is far more likely to stick. It should come as no surprise that inductive learning is much preferred by educationalists. It is also worth noting that the testimony to the failure of traditional Christian pulpit teaching to remain in the conscious memory until the end of Sunday is more frequent than we would care to admit.

Insofar as we look at narrative preaching based on the narrative passages of the Bible, a further advantage of the approach is the way that it engages the imagination. Because our lives are lived out as our own personal stories narrative is an amazingly effective medium of communication. It is both intuitive and empathetic. It speaks directly to our own experience of life and we understand. We recognise ourselves, our struggles and our delights in the stories of others. Characters from the stories we hear come to live in our imagination. As an avid fan of *Star Trek: The Next Generation*, Captain Jean Luc Pickard and Commander Ryker will live in my memory forever.

It may well be that introducing a narrative style of preaching to a congregation may give a more balanced pattern of teaching and preaching. Studies in the function of the human brain appear to indicate that the left hemisphere controls the rational, logical and sequential thought processes. This is where the Christian church has concentrated in its preaching over the years. The right hemisphere, however, seems to be responsible for our intuitive, holistic and imagistic thought processes.[2] Using both deductive and inductive approaches will ensure that the preacher engages with the whole person as well as not marginalising those with either an artistic or rational orientation.

So, what does it mean to preach in a narrative style? What do narrative style sermons look like? Three main forms of sermon need to occupy our attention:

1. Where the preacher is the narrator of the story – a third-person narrative.
2. Where the preacher is a character in the story – a first-person narrative.
3. Where the preacher uses a narrative form with non-narrative material.
4. The common element to each of them is the form or style they take, the plot.

The Homiletical Plot and the 'Lowry Loop'

One of the most influential contributors to the renaissance of narrative in preaching is Eugene Lowry, for over thirty years Professor of Preaching at Saint Paul School of Theology in Kansas City, Missouri, and an ordained minister of the United Methodist Church. Lowry's landmark contribution was his 1980 book, *The Homiletical Plot: The Sermon as a Narrative Art Form*.

---

[2] Pierre Babin, *The New Era in Religious Communication*, 55 and Jensen, *Thinking in Story*, 27, 41.

Seeking to understand and articulate what makes a 'good' sermon from the perspective of the pew, rather than the text book, he makes the point that the parable of the Prodigal Son would have looked very different if Jesus had organised it according to its logical ingredients rather than the journey of the son.[3] As a consequence, he explores and advocates an approach he considers to be more in keeping with the biblical text:

> Plot! This is the key term for a reshaped image of the sermon. Preaching is storytelling. A sermon is a narrative art form.[4]

Accepting that a plot moves from problem to solution; from tension to resolution, Lowry observes that this movement, of necessity, shapes the form of the sermon. He therefore suggests that the plot line of a narrative-style sermon should move through five basic steps or transitions.[5] To each of these transitions he ascribes an abbreviated title that clearly indicates its role in the overall development of the homiletical plot:

1. Upsetting the equilibrium – *Oops*.
2. Analysing the discrepancy – *Ugh*.
3. Disclosing the clue to resolution – *Aha*.
4. Experiencing the gospel – *Whee*.
5. Anticipating the consequences – *Yeah*.

---

[3] Eugene L. Lowry, *The Homiletical Plot: The Sermon as Narrative Art Form*, 12.

[4] Lowry, *Homiletical Plot*, 15.

[5] Lowry accepts that there are many different ways to construct a plot and its moves, however, he does consider what follows to be an appropriate model for the preacher and the homiletical task, cf. Lowry, *Homiletical Plot*, 22–5.

He represents this diagrammatically, as illustrated below, with what we might call the 'Lowry Loop'.

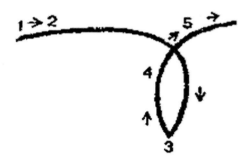

The "Lowry Loop"

The sense of movement that a narrative plot brings is immediately obvious from the diagram. A plot begins in one place and ends up at another. This is because a plot-driven sermon takes its listeners on a journey in a way that is not true of more traditional sermons which will tend to stay 'in one place' as the truth in a passage is explored, a doctrinal position is argued for or a moral standard is upheld and defended.

In exploring what preaching in a narrative style looks and feels like it is important to understand how this idea of plot development works. The 'Lowry Loop' provides a helpful model to work with.

Upsetting the equilibrium – the 'Oops!'

At the beginning of every sermon the preacher needs to capture the congregation's imagination. For many years I have always worked hard at the openings for my sermons. While there are some saints who will listen with wrapt attention to whatever is said, others have to be helped to engage and focus on the subject to hand. One experienced preacher warned me at the outset of my preaching career that, 'If you haven't got them with you in the first minute and a half, you've effectively lost them for the whole of the sermon.'

Narrative-style preaching works by creating and using tension to hold people's attention. For Lowry this upsetting of the equilibrium at the beginning of a sermon is the essential 'hook' that enables people to connect with the preacher's theme. In many ways it is similar to the opening scene of a film. Walt Disney's *Jungle Book* begins with the narrator's statement that many strange things happen in the jungle followed by the sound of a baby crying. The tension is established and questions are raised that need to be answered and will prove to be central to the plot of the film. What is a baby doing in the jungle? How did it get there? It's in danger, how will it survive? By contrast, in the first of the Wachowski brothers' *Matrix Trilogy* a well staged chase scene as the character Trinity seeks to escape from the Matrix provides the initial suspense in an extremely compelling manner. This chase itself is incidental to the story that will unfold, but wider questions sit beneath the action.

Few sermons can compete with a Hollywood blockbuster, but the principle is the same. However, preachers are at a disadvantage. Frequently we have been taught to make our presentations in the manner of the academy rather than as entertainers. To present a logical argument we introduce our theme by telling the audience what we are about to tell them; we tell them it; and then we conclude by telling them what we have told them in a final reprise. Agatha Christie would not have sold many detective novels if she had revealed in the opening chapter who did it. Yet traditional preaching has taught us to give away the plot at the outset. Adopting a narrative style in the pulpit requires a different approach. Tension has to be created at the outset and not released until much later in the sermon. It seems to be a basic facet of human psychology that we need to resolve ambiguity and release tension, 'don't keep me in suspense'. It is a strong compulsion and often we can feel the incompleteness. Like a piece of music that ends with an incomplete chord, we are left hanging. This is a powerful strategy for getting and keeping listeners' attention.

In addressing a story from the Bible there might be any one of a number of ways in which the initial tension could be established and disequilibrium potentially created in the minds of a congregation. The story of the Samaritan Woman at the Well in John 4 is loaded with possibilities, here are three:

- *Racism* (v. 9) – the woman is surprised at Jesus because he does not conform to accepted patterns of behaviour with regard to their nationalities.
- *Marriage and cohabitation* (vv. 16–17) – with five marriages behind her the woman is cohabiting with her present partner. Jesus does not condemn her for it and uses her that same day as an evangelist to bring her whole community to hear him.
- *Gender issues* (v. 27) – when the disciples returned from getting supplies in Sychar they were surprised to find him talking with a woman.

Analysing the discrepancy – the 'Ugh!'

In this second stage of a narrative-style sermon the content is determined by analysis. The examination of the discrepancy that was established in the opening section now becomes central to the development of the plot. At the outset it is important to note that, in terms of length, this part of the sermon can be as long as all the other elements put together as it sets up the whole sermon and the application of the gospel that is to follow.

The single most important question to be addressed is the question, 'Why?' In the story of the woman at the well, for example, we might ask:

- Why did Jesus engage the woman in conversation and yet speak in riddles?
- When she responds positively to the 'living water' image why does Jesus raise the issue of her failed relationships and then fail to help her see that cohabitation is not a godly lifestyle?
- Why did she raise the subject of **whose** 'holy place' is the most appropriate location to worship God?

There are other questions that could be asked too, but the 'oops' turns into an 'ugh' because of the movement in the plot development of this section of the sermon. In it the preacher seeks to demonstrate that there is a lot more going on in the story than we initially thought. Upon examination the issues are discovered to be more involved and far more complicated than had been anticipated at first sight. Indeed, some have suggested that this part of sermon development is not only to establish an 'ugh' response in our listeners, but then to go on and 'make the ugh ughier'!

Analysing the discrepancy establishes what is wrong. What is the problem, the bind, the ambiguity that needs to be resolved? If preaching is about proclaiming a gospel of good news, what exactly is it that we need to hear some genuinely good news about? In essence, this is a diagnostic task. Of course, diagnostic failure can be fatal in sermon preparation. Failure to diagnose correctly presenting symptoms in a doctor's surgery can lead to inappropriate treatment and, at best, the absence of any improvement in the patient. However, inappropriate treatment can also make things much worse. The same dynamics are at work in both preaching and pastoral ministry. Indeed, the two are inextricably intertwined. Almost every sermon has pastoral implications. For the good news of the gospel to have its full effect bringing healing, hope and spiritual life to its hearers requires a diagnosis that enables a proper application of the gospel to be made.

Structuring a sermon to follow the development of a plot requires a preacher to think differently. If tension is created that captures the attention of a congregation in the first part of the sermon, it is important not to throw it away during the analysis. Actually the tension should be heightened. A different strategy needs to be followed in the writing of the sermon. The more traditional practice of researching a subject and sharing the conclusions reached in a sermon should be set to one side. In a narrative-style sermon the preacher shares with a congregation not only the conclusions of their research but also the whole process of discovery, including the blind alleys and false trails that ultimately lead to the conclusion; a conclusion that is held in reserve to the very last moment.

Take, for example, a crime thriller, where the attention of the audience is held by wanting to know 'who did it'. One of my favourite detectives is the medieval monk, Brother Cadfael from the Ellis Peters novels. The stories are set in the city of Shrewsbury and the Abbey church and monastery of St Peter and St Paul. As the herbalist monk explores the evidence, examines the characters and discovers new clues, the plot unfolds and moves inexorably towards solving the crime – almost always a murder. Like any good novelist, Peters helps the reader to make premature conclusions only to dismiss them, while at the same time building the body of evidence that will ultimately lead to the miscreant who should have been spotted from the outset.

Lowry observes that the greatest single weakness of the average sermon is a weakness in diagnosis.[6] The temptation for a preacher is to substitute depth of analysis for description or illustration without even being aware of it. It is a temptation because it is an easier path to follow in preparing the sermon.

When we succumb to the temptation to only be descriptive of a passage it leaves us with only a rudimentary or superficial level of analysis of what is going on in the story. The ability of our preaching to connect with the life and experience of our listeners is thereby severely limited. For example, let's look at the layers of analysis we can make to the question, why did the woman go to the well?

- The simple descriptive answer is
  … because she needed water.
- A first level of analysis would indicate that
  … she went on her own in the heat of midday to avoid people because she had a bad reputation.
- A further level of analysis might explore
  … why we avoid people and the hurtfulness of rejection that makes you want to hide away.
- To take the analysis even further it is legitimate to examine
  … the long-term impact on the woman and her self-image of her failed relationships and being an object of local scorn.

The temptation to use biblical stories illustratively is also a strong one. At one level, this is both understandable and legitimate as we want the biblical text to provide us with our models of behaviour and practice. However, when we

---

[6] Lowry, *Homiletical Plot*, 38–9.

use the scriptural stories illustratively without any depth of analysis we succeed in robbing them of their power to speak into people's lives, offering only 'pat' and shallow application from the riches to be found in the text. To turn once more to the story of the woman at the well, it is an amazing example of someone witnessing to their community about their encounter with Jesus. Again, the greater the depth of the analysis the more helpful the story becomes.

- As a simple illustration a preacher might say
  ... the woman met with Jesus and then told all of her neighbours and friends about it and brought them to him. So should we.
- Analysis of the woman's response begins to ask the question why she did what she did. A first level of analysis might pick up that
  ... when Jesus had revealed himself to her as the Messiah the revelatory experience compelled her to share the good news of her discovery.
- Taking the process of analysis further we might explore some of the other dynamics of this encounter and the impact they had upon the woman.
  ... Here was someone who other people scorned that Jesus took time with; he brought her history of failed relationships with her ex-husbands into the open and yet did not condemn her for it; he effectively dealt with any sense of racial superiority/inferiority in the conversation about worship; and any sense she had of being a second-class person because of her gender was also set aside. Here was someone who had turned her world and her experience on its head. It was an affirming, liberating, amazing experience to meet Jesus. It is hardly surprising that she had to tell the people she lived with about it all.

Lowry says it well when he describes the responsibility of the preacher in analysing the discrepancy in the following terms:

> Our responsibility in preaching the gospel requires us to probe behind the behaviour to motives, fears, and needs in order to ascertain the cause or causes ... The purpose of the sermonic process of analysis is to uncover the areas of interior motivation where the problem is generated, and hence to expose the motivational setting toward which any cure will need to be directed.[7]

This is easily said and much more difficult to put into practice, but no one said preaching would be easy. It requires a strong measure of self and interpersonal awareness on the part of the preacher. We have to be students of the human heart, voracious in our appetite to understand people and what makes them tick. Rita was a mentor to me in spiritual things in the early days of my ministry. I remember one time after I had preached my heart out that she took me aside and said:

> Roger, it is a sobering thing for a preacher to remember that you only see in others what you have already seen in yourself. As a preacher you have to know your own heart before God because you can only take people as far in the spiritual life as you have gone yourself.

The depth and precision of our analysis determines how we apply the gospel to those elements of the human condition that we are addressing. If it remains superficial, so will our preaching. If it has depth and relevance the Holy Spirit will use it to touch people's hearts and transform their lives as they are brought into conformity with Christ.

---

[7] Lowry, *Homiletical Plot*, 40.

Disclosing the clue to resolution – the 'Aha!'

This is a pivotal element in the progression of a plot and it signals the beginning of the end. The entire sermon has been pressing towards this point, probing the question why? Yet the key to resolving the problem and relieving the tension of the plot is not evident to this point. However, once this information is disclosed it is as if a light goes on. Now you can see, hence the 'Aha!' Often called 'the reversal' because of the radical way in which the disclosure turns everything upside down and brings a fresh perspective to bear on the problem, it is frequently a surprise and from an unexpected quarter. It is a 'EUREKA!' moment.

In the story of Jesus meeting the Samaritan woman from Sychar in John 4 we have already seen that her race (v. 9), her lifestyle (vv. 16–18) and her gender (v. 27) would appear to have disqualified her from entering into a meaningful conversation with a religious teacher like Jesus. The reversal is contained in the conversation about which mountain is the best place to worship God. Jesus turns the subject from a potential discussion about the relative merits of two holy places of worship to the two qualities of worship for which God looks in true worshippers. In doing so he makes his position clear: 'true worshippers will worship the Father in spirit and in truth for they are the kind of worshippers the Father seeks' (v. 23).

If these are the prerequisites for true worship then there is no place for any notion that nationality, past moral failure or even gender as disqualifying criteria from engaging with the Lord. Jesus' conversation with the woman therefore has its explanation. Yet because of our cultural distance from the first century it would be easy to underplay the way this particular reversal in the plot runs counter to accepted truth. We read through twenty-first century eyes. The Jews did believe themselves to be 'God's chosen people' and that the Samaritans were inferior. Great store was placed on the righteousness that was according to the law and the Pharisees were the guardians of the holiness of the people. Women, of course, were not allowed to worship with the men and some even doubted that they had souls.

Lowry likens the reversal to pulling the rug out from under a listening congregation. He quotes with approval the narrative theorist William Foster Harris: 'The method of solution invariably is to invert, to reverse, to 'twist' the problem picture so that a new picture abruptly emerges.'[8]

Clearly, Jesus understood the power of the reversal as he frequently used it in his parables. The parables of the Unmerciful Servant, the Labourers in the Vineyard, the Good Samaritan, the Rich Fool, the Prodigal Son and the Pharisee and the Tax Collector are illustrative of this strand in Jesus' teaching (Mt. 18:23–35; 20:1–16; Lk. 10:25–37; 12:13–21; 15:11–32; 18:9–14). Indeed, at times reversal seems to be a fundamental principle of the kingdom of God. Accepted truth is turned upside down with the recognition that you must lose your life to save it, that the last will be first, that the leader must be the servant of all and that adults must become like little children to enter the kingdom (Mk. 10:15, 42–44; Lk. 9:24; 13:30).

Lowry's rug must be carefully laid given that so many of the biblical stories, especially the parables of Jesus, are already so well known. To have the same impact on a contemporary audience will often require the cultivation of the kind of assumptions that would be in the minds of Jesus' listeners before he pulled his reversal. Sometimes it may even involve a recreating of the context that would not be readily apparent today. Kenneth Bailey talks about the problem of the 'cultural foreignness' that we encounter as we study the Gospels. Through careful research from ancient and

---

[8] Lowry, *Homiletical Plot*, 56.

modern sources he provides a way for the contemporary student of Jesus to get back inside the text.[9]

With the clue to the resolution of the discrepancy disclosed a new door is opened for the proclamation of the gospel.

Experiencing the gospel – the 'Whee!'

Once the clue to the resolution of the tension is revealed the listeners are ready to experience the gospel. One of the advantages of using the narrative style is that it engages the emotions. A range of feelings from empathy to the intensity of past personal experience can be evoked so that listening to the sermon is not merely an intellectual experience. Members of a congregation may literally 'feel' the good news of the gospel as it is proclaimed and applied.

The hard work in identifying an accurate diagnosis of the problem now bears its dividend. What has gone before is crucial at this point of the sermon. Jesus spoke of his mission using a medical analogy when he responded to the Pharisees and the teachers of the law saying, 'It is not the healthy who need a doctor, but the sick. I have not come to call the righteous, but sinners to repentance' (Lk. 5:31–32).

He knew exactly what he was doing in attending the banquet at Levi's house and why he was doing it. It is important for the preacher to have the same measure of clarity at this point of the sermon. There must be consistency between the issues raised through the analysis of the discrepancy and the good news of the gospel that is now applied.

With the return of the disciples to the well outside of the town of Sychar the woman who has been speaking with Jesus concludes her conversation and returns home,

---

[9] Kenneth Bailey, *Poet and Peasant: A Literary-cultural Approach to the Parables in Luke*, 27.

leaving her water jar behind anxious to tell all her neighbours about this amazing man she had met! What had got into her? What had happened?

The clue to the good news she had experienced is in what she tells them, 'Come, see a man who told me everything I ever did. Could this be the Christ?' (Jn. 4:29). It was not the conversation about water, holy places or even the key insights about worship that had done it for the woman. It was the fact that Jesus knew who she was and what she was, he knew of her shameful and failed past experience in relationship with men, yet still he talked with her. He gave her respect and dignity. He was a man and a Jew, she was a woman and a Samaritan and that made no difference either. In the one phrase is summed up the inclusive generosity and acceptance of the grace of God. No wonder she was bursting to tell others. The woman who had constantly experienced the hurtful rejection and scorn from others, who had a painfully low self-image due to her inability to get her life together had been given hope through this conversation. The fact that the phrase relating to her personal experience is repeated in verse 40 underlines its significance in the narrative. It is hardly surprising then to find that this experience of God's loving kindness that Jesus demonstrated had got her asking the right theological questions too.

Lowry points out how clearly the Word can be heard once the reversal has made ready the context. He also notes how fatal to the whole endeavour it would be if the gospel truth were announced at the outset. It is important for the congregation to first experience the discrepancy before they can fully understand the release of the gospel.[10]

---

[10] Lowry, *Homiletical Plot*, 63.

Anticipating the consequences – the 'Yeah!'

At the climax point of the reversal in the plot the tension built up in the first two-thirds to three-quarters of the sermon is released and then rapidly dissipates. This final section establishes closure on the preaching event and the necessary denouement for the narrative.[11]

What are the consequences in the narrative itself for the event that has been recounted? What lies in the future? What can be expected? What should be done? What is now possible?

The story of the meeting between the woman and Jesus just outside the town of Sychar has its own conclusion. Jesus is invited by the townspeople to stay around for two further days on the basis of the woman's testimony. When Jesus comes to move on they make a simple statement of faith: 'They said to the woman, "We no longer believe just because of what you said; now we have heard for ourselves, and we know that this man really is the Saviour of the world"' (Jn. 4:42).

The progression is clear. The woman's witness to what had happened when she met Jesus aroused their interest. Having met Jesus for themselves they too had come to see him for who he was, the Messiah and Saviour of the world, and this was now their own personal faith. Closure is affected and John simply adds that after two days Jesus left for Galilee.

Lowry makes an interesting theological point on the nature of preaching in a narrative style. In a more traditionally styled sermon the climax comes towards the end with the appeal for a response at the close of the sermon. In the

---

[11] Denouement: literally the final resolution or clarification of a dramatic or narrative plot, from the French dénouement, *an untying.*

narrative style the climax comes at the point of the reversal and therefore, rather than being focused on the human centred response to the gospel it sits with the decisive activity of God contained in the reversal.[12]

Having charted the development of a plot-based sermon through the model provided by the 'Lowry Loop' there are two further things that ought to be noted.

First, there is no doubt that in the dynamics of a narrative style sermon the function of tension is a key ingredient. It is interesting to identify exactly what is happening to the tension during the progress of a sermon's plot.

1. Upsetting the equilibrium – *tension established.*
2. Analysing the discrepancy – *tension intensified.*
3. Disclosing the clue to resolution – *tension released.*
4. Experiencing the gospel – *the release of tension enjoyed.*
5. Anticipating the consequences – *tension resolved.*

Secondly, it is important to realise that when dealing with a narrative passage of the Bible where the plot is clearly identifiable, as with the example from John 4, the preacher does not necessarily have to follow the plot development of the text in the plot development of the sermon. Clearly, they would be closely related as the material in the biblical text remains the same. However, it is legitimate to select one of the subsidiary themes and use that to base the plot of the sermon around. John 4 is rich with potential themes and racism, sexism and the marriage/cohabitation debate have already been identified. To these could be added the personal encounter with Christ, acceptable worship and spiritual energy among a number of others. For each of

---

[12] Lowry, *Homiletical Plot*, 68–9.

these, the development of the sermon plot and its use of the
biblical text would be nuanced differently.

Three Types of Narrative Sermon

*When the preacher is the narrator of the story – a third
person narrative*

In a third-person narrative sermon the preacher acts as the
narrator of the story. It is actually a style that is clearly in
harmony with the Bible as most biblical stories are written
from this perspective.

As in any narration, the Bible included, the narrator
knows all, sees all and understands all while only revealing
the necessary details. There can be no doubt that it feels like
a very different way to preach. The first time I attempted to
preach a narrative sermon I chose the story of Saul's ascend-
ing to the kingship in Israel in 1 Samuel 9 – 10.[13] I was glad
that I had taken the advice that had been offered and had
committed the script to memory as one of my first reflections afterwards was that it would have been very difficult if
I had not. This was for two particular reasons.

First, I found myself, unexpectedly acting out the narrative as I preached it. I normally walk about when I preach
and this much I expected. But as I told of how Saul was hiding in the baggage pile I found myself squatting down close
to the ground. When he encountered the group of travelling
prophets and was overcome by the Spirit and began to
dance and move with the beat and rhythm of their music, I
found myself doing a little impromptu jig!

Secondly, it quickly became clear to me that this was a far
more intimate and free-flowing genre of preaching. To be

---

[13] The text of this first attempt at a third person narrative is included in Chapter 7.

struggling with notes or separated from the congregation by a pulpit or lectern would have been inhibiting and a distraction. Whether large prompt cards at the back of the church would work, I have yet to try.

The role of the narrator is to enable their listeners to begin to imagine and live inside a different world. This requires a disciplined approach on a number of levels. Thorough research is helpful in enabling a picture to be painted of what it was like. Engaging the senses quickly allows people to understand and experience what you are describing. Taste, smell, sight, sound and sensations are wonderful gateways to a different world. However, as vivid as the picture may be it only takes one anachronism to destroy it. An anachronism is a mistake of time. In our normal preaching we shoot back and forth between the biblical world and our own. However, when a narrative sermon is dealing with a biblical story such liberties are not easily possible.

I remember a friend preaching on the rape of Tamar by Amnon. This was a powerful passage that he had opened up skillfully, helping us to understand sibling rivalry and some of the other subplots that were running in the story. However, seeking to lighten things with a little humour he mixed the ancient world with a modern idiom. He referred on one occasion to 'used camel dealers' and on another to a male fragrance called 'essence of donkey'. We handled the first reference but collapsed into hysterical laughter at the second. As funny as it was, the moment was lost because it did not fit. Anachronism does not work.

There is always the question of how to conclude a narrative sermon. Do you finish the story and leave it there or do you then move on to explicitly apply the truths that you have been seeking to communicate? There are differences of opinion among those who are experienced in narrative preaching.

On the one side are those who argue that one of the most powerful strengths of a narrative preaching style is the inductive manner in which it communicates. To move into a direct application undermines this.[14]

On the other side, many preachers have found it to be a helpful adjunct to the narrative sermon and are keen not to lose an opportunity to apply the Scriptures. However, those who do move to explicit application need to recognise the delicate nature of the medium of narrative preaching. Pause for a few moments, then come out of character and move to a different location to address the congregation and thereby underline that you are now speaking as yourself. Then keep the application both light and brief. My own personal conviction would be to conclude the narrative and leave it at that.

When the preacher is a character in the story – a first-person narrative

If a first-person narrative is to be attempted the first question is which character to become. Essentially there are three main options, to be one of the main characters, a named minor character or a fictional observer.

Having chosen the character the next decision is whether to be in costume or not. Costumed preaching is very unusual in the UK and would raise eyebrows in most churches on any given Sunday. By contrast, it is much more common in the USA and has an honoured tradition having been practised by accomplished and well-respected preachers.

First-person narratives clearly rely far more on a preacher's acting ability as it is necessary to 'get into character' and preach from a perspective that is not your own. One

---

[14] Major Mike Parker of the Salvation Army has an interesting reflection from his own experience on this issue in Chapter 10.

significant difference from a third-person narrative is the issue of perspective. Where a narrator is omniscient, a character that is personally part of a narrative can only have the limited knowledge and understanding which the particular character in the story would have.

Much of what applies to a third-person narrative sermon also applies to sermons in the first person. Issues of movement, anachronism and application are generally the same, though coming out of character needs to be more carefully executed, especially if the preacher is in costume.

When the preacher uses a narrative form with a non-narrative subject

This is simply using the insights of narrative theory in general and plot development in particular to provide a different kind of sermon structure to that which might be more traditionally deployed. It remains an inductive form that utilises tension to keep a congregation engaged with the message. However, other than requiring a preacher to work to a different structure with its implications for writing and delivery, a preacher can continue in much the same way as they normally do week by week.

Some Objections to Preaching in a Narrative Style

It's not really preaching, it's only storytelling

There is a great tradition of storytelling from which the church has benefited enormously over the years. In Britain it is experiencing something of a renaissance. *The Telling Place* initiative which was founded in 1998 as a collaboration between Bible Society and the Northumbria Community is illustrative of this. Part of its mission statement is to 'Engage with and impact culture by telling God's Story and helping the Church rediscover the power of storytelling.'

However, narrative preaching is not storytelling, though clearly there are similarities and areas of overlap. In the introduction to this book, I identified five principles that are foundational for Christian preaching. They are each directly applicable to the narrative style.

The Primacy of Preaching (the missiological imperative) – this identified the primary role preaching had in the ministry and calling of Jesus. As we have seen, he often used what we would now identify as insights from narrative theory in his preaching, especially in the parables.

Preaching the Word of God (the biblical word) – a frequent concern with narrative preaching is how far it is based on the creative imagination of the preacher to fill in the gaps left by the text. In truth, narrative sermons are like any other sermon and, how close they are to the text of Scripture depends upon the preacher. As Haddon Robinson, an American professor of preaching, has observed, 'Truth and interpretation, history and imagination are woven into every sermon.'[15] Ultimately, it is the responsibility of every preacher to ensure that their sermons are thoroughly biblical.

Truth through personality (the incarnate word) – as we have seen the role of the preacher as the mediator of the analysis is determinative and indispensable.

Audience focused (the contextualised word) – one of the major strengths of the narrative-style approach is in the power of its application coming out of the analysis of the human condition.

---

[15] Haddon W. Robinson and Torrey W. Robinson, *It's All in How You Tell It: Preaching First-person Expository Messages,* 73.

Collaboration with the Holy Spirit (the inspired word) – preaching is Spirit illumined and Spirit empowered proclamation. Narrative-style preaching is gospel proclamation that has at its heart the objective of individuals experiencing the good news of the gospel of Jesus.

It's all about structure and it is not really spiritual at all

Certainly a great deal of what is involved in learning to preach in a narrative style is about learning new ways of approaching the task of preaching. Much of this has to do with the structure and organisation of our material. However, it would be a naïve error to conclude that it was unspiritual merely because there was concentration on structure when normally preachers do not have to think about structure at all. In reality every preacher has a way of organising their material. It may be a discipline that was learned or a skill that has been grown intuitively, but it is there either way. The narrative form is just a different way of organising and structuring material. Because it may be new to us we will be particularly aware of the mechanics until it becomes more like second nature. However, this does not make it less spiritual. As we have seen it is thoroughly biblical. Surely the only question would be whether it enables the Holy Spirit to speak more clearly into the hearts and minds of those who listen to us preach or not.

It's not real preaching that opens up the Bible to us and explains it.

It is particularly challenging for a congregation that is used to traditional expository preaching to come to terms with narrative-style preaching. The move from a strongly deductive and logical presentation to a wholeheartedly inductive approach that is intuitive is a big one – it just 'feels' all wrong.

The Bible does not actually prescribe acceptable and unacceptable sermon forms. The deductive model with which we are all familiar owes more to Greco-Roman rhetoric than it does to the biblical tradition. There is no eleventh commandment that states, 'Thou shalt preach only expository sermons!'

Using the effectiveness of narrative to communicate is resting on worldly wisdom rather than the power of the Holy Spirit.

A wise older minister once said to me, 'Roger, never forget that all truth is God's truth because there is nothing in this world of ours that he did not set in being.' We have already seen in an earlier chapter how central narrative and story are to the world in which we live. God created it this way. If the principles of narrative show us an effective way to communicate the gospel a way in which some of the obstacles that might normally be present can be removed, I'm all for giving it a go. As the apostle Paul said to the Corinthians:

> What then is my reward? Just this: that in preaching the gospel I may offer it free of charge, and so not make use of my rights in preaching it. Though I am free and belong to no man, I make myself a slave to everyone, to win as many as possible. To the Jews I became like a Jew, to win the Jews. To those under the law I became like one under the law (though I myself am not under the law), so as to win those under the law. To those not having the law I became like one not having the law (though I am not free from God's law but am under Christ's law), so as to win those not having the law. To the weak I became weak, to win the weak. I have become all things to all men so that by all possible means I might save some. I do all this for the sake of the gospel that I may share in its blessings.
>
> (1 Cor. 9:18–23).

5

Researching, Writing and Delivering a Narrative Sermon

'Old habits die hard', at least that's what the proverb says. The truth is that for many of us as preachers the regular round of weekly preaching has formed very entrenched habits of practice in how we prepare and write our sermons. Narrative preaching requires us to break with these habits and take the risk of doing things in a new way. Just because we need to approach the biblical text from a different angle, ask different questions of it and ultimately write our sermon according to a different set of criteria, it is not any the less spiritual or authentically Christian as a consequence. It is merely different, and that difference makes us far more self-conscious and aware of the mechanics of what we are doing when compared with our normal experience.

Throughout the whole of the process of researching, writing and delivering a narrative sermon remember that this is a spiritual discipline. The underlying questions remain, 'What is God saying through this text?' and 'What does God want me to preach in this sermon?'

What follows will explore the practicalities of the process of researching, writing and delivering a narrative sermon. This will be accomplished by using the major elements of narrative identified in Chapter 3 to both explore the biblical text and prepare the sermon.[1] To illustrate the processes involved, each section will also include the underlying preparation for the example of the first-person sermon, 'You'll never believe this!' that opens Chapter 8 and is based on Acts 2:1–41.

Researching a Narrative Sermon

Initial preparation

Before you get down to the exegetical work that is necessary to begin to write the sermon, sit down with the selected narrative and begin with the text itself. Treat the story as a story and read it as you would any other novel or biography. Ignore any chapter and verse divisions and keep reading until the story is brought to an appropriate closure. Then read it a second time with a notepad and jot down anything in particular that has caught your attention. What are the things that you would like to know more about? It might be that something in the setting has struck you and you do not know how it would work out in practice. On the other hand, it may be that a character has referred to some other incident of which you are unaware and you need to follow it up. Do this before you refer to any biblical commentaries or reference books.

Sample sermon preparation – Acts 2:1–41

   1.   A 'sound like' the blowing of a violent wind plus what 'seemed to be' tongues of fire. What was the experience

---

[1] Paul Borden outlines an alternate exegetical methodology in, 'Is there really one big idea in that story,' in Keith Willhite and Scott M. Gibson, *The Big Idea of Biblical Preaching*, 67–80. It is also summarised in Robinson and Robinson, *How You Tell It*, 140–1.

like that sits behind these seemingly inadequate attempts to explain it?

2. If they were in the upper room of the house prior to the Spirit coming, why is there no record of them leaving the room before the crowd forms and Peter preaches?

3. Speaking of Jesus' ministry and death (vv. 22–23), 'as you yourselves know', 'handed over to you', 'and you … put him to death'. Of course, the last time many of this group of pilgrims were together in Jerusalem was at Passover. They were, therefore, personal witnesses to the climax of Jesus' ministry and his execution.

4. Where in Jerusalem do you get sufficient water to baptise by immersion three thousand people at one time? How did they know that it was that number?

5. What must it have been like at the end of the day for the disciples? Suddenly, things had come alive in a way that they cannot have anticipated, but for which they were now responsible.

Mapping the story

Seek to get inside the story by identifying the main sections and transitions. Chart it on a sheet of paper with one sentence for each section or transition.

How is the story designed? Is it told in the first or third person? Who is the narrator? Is the story told straightforwardly or does it use flashback and/or foreshadowing? Is it possible to identify a plot in the narrative? What is emphasised?

Sample sermon preparation

1. The main sections/transitions are:
   • The coming of the Holy Spirit (vv. 1–4).
   • The representatives of the nations hear the wonders of God in their own languages (vv. 5–12).

- Some in the crowd think that the disciples are drunk (v. 13).
- Peter preaches a sermon to explain what is happening (vv. 14–36), including quotes from Joel (vv. 17–21) and David (vv. 25–28).
- The crowd respond by asking 'what shall we do?' (v. 37).
- Peter calls for repentance and baptism for the forgiveness of sins and as precursors of the gift of the Holy Spirit (vv. 38–39).
- The end of the sermon is summarised (v. 40).
- Three thousand accept the message and are baptised (v. 41).

2. The narrative is told in the third person by Luke.
3. The story of the Day of Pentecost is told straightforwardly, though Peter does include flashbacks to Jesus' ministry, execution and resurrection.
4. It is difficult to identify a plot solely from this passage. However, if the story begins at the beginning of Acts with Jesus' charge for the disciples to be his witnesses throughout the world, and then continues with them safe behind locked doors, fearful of what might happen to them, there is the creation of turbulence and disequilibrium at the outset. How will this group accomplish that? Then the reception of the Holy Spirit becomes the reversal as Peter preaches with boldness and the three thousand new, baptised believers is the denouement of the plot.
5. Five things appear to me to be particularly emphasised in the narrative:
    1. The disciples being filled with the Holy Spirit at the beginning of the passage.
    2. The roll-call of the nations who all heard the wonders of God in their own language.

3. The accusation of being drunk is then immediately answered by Peter at the beginning of his preaching. This must count as a narrative repetition.
4. The question, 'what shall we do?' with the answer to repent, be baptised, receiving both forgiveness and the gift of the Holy Spirit.
5. The three thousand who were baptised and added to the embryonic Christian community.

Exploring the setting

Setting is about where and when the narrative takes place. Some clues will be in the narrative, or questions will be begged by the events themselves. The cultural, historical and geographical information that can be supplied for the setting helps to bring colour and depth to a presentation as well as understanding. Biblical encyclopaedias, atlases and dictionaries can be of enormous benefit in supplementing the information gleaned from commentaries on the text itself.

Acts 2:1–41

Time – the festival of Pentecost, a kind of Jewish Harvest Festival. It was a pilgrimage feast to which thousands were drawn.

Location – Jerusalem, but probably not beginning in the upper room. Rather, the location for all the events is on Temple Mount. The evidence is:

- 'When the day of Pentecost came, they were all together in one place ...' (v. 1). This would be the Temple as it was a festival day and they were in Jerusalem. Where else would they be?

- The sound of the wind filled 'the whole house' where they were sitting (v. 2). Not the upper room of the house in 1:13 but, 'the house' built by Solomon referred to in 7:47. 'The house' is an attested local contraction of 'the house of the Lord' at the time.

- There is no mention of the disciples leaving the house to go out among the crowd following their filling by the Holy Spirit. Rather, a crowd gathers around them, attracted by the unusual linguistic phenomenon (v. 6). This is normal crowd dynamics that we witness today.

- The size of the crowd listening to Peter preach has to have a minimum size of three thousand, supposing that everyone who listened got baptised. The likelihood is that the crowd was much larger than this. Given the **cramped nature of Jerusalem, the only space large** enough to take such a crowd inside the city would have been the outer court of the Temple.

- Water to baptise three thousand would not have been easy to find. However, excavations at Temple Mount in the 1960s discovered rows of ritual Mikva at the foot of the southern approach. These were ritual baths in which worshippers immersed themselves before proceeding to worship. Looking much like mini-Baptist baptisteries, these Mikva were readily to hand for those who wished to respond to Peter's call to be baptised. It is interesting to note that flowing or 'living' water was channelled to these Mikva from the Kidron, and worshippers used them by immersing themselves having removed their clothing.[2]

---

[2] I am particularly indebted to Dr R. Stephen Notley, Professor of Biblical Studies at the New York City campus of Nyack College. In the early 1990s Steve was resident in Jerusalem working on his PhD., 'The Concept of the Holy Spirit in Jewish Literature of the Second Commonwealth and Pre-Pauline Christianity' at

Architecture of the city and Temple – it is important to be able to visualise the local architecture to get inside the story. The Temple was an imposing structure of vast open space when compared to the more basic and close confined structures of an ancient city.

Identifying the characters in the narrative

The individuals who are identified in the text are key contributors to the development of a narrative. Who are they? How are they characterised? How does the author seek to deepen their characterisation through action, dialogue and comment?

Sample sermon preparation

1. The only named character is the disciple Peter. Throughout the passage he is clearly identified as acting as part of the wider group. In verse 1 they were 'all together in one place'; in verse 14 when he begins to preach, 'Then Peter stood up with the Eleven'; and when the crowd respond to his preaching they address the group, 'Brothers, what shall we do?' rather than just addressing the preacher. Characterisation is not extensive in this passage though there are a number of indicators that can be identified:
   - Clearly, there is a transformation in Peter from the fearfulness of the upper room to the confident practice of public speaking before a huge crowd and openly professing faith.
   - In his preaching, Peter comes across as biblically literate in his use of quotes from Joel and David (vv. 17–28).

---

[2] (*Continued*) the Hebrew University of Jerusalem. It was there that we met and he took me through these exciting insights into the location of the birth of the church.

- The preaching is also affecting as many of his hearers are 'cut to the heart' (v. 37).
- There is also a note of emotional engagement as he pleads with the crowd, 'Save yourselves ...' (v. 40).
- From wider references in the Gospels we know that Peter was big-hearted, impulsive and at times even hot-headed. He had a tendency to open his mouth without thinking about the consequences and had been known to lack the resolve to stick with his convictions (Cf. Mt. 14:28–30; 16:13–23; Lk. 22:54–62; Jn 13:1–10; Gal. 2:11–14).

2. The two other characters who speak are anonymous individuals who speak on behalf of the crowd. The first accuses the disciples of having drunk too much wine (v. 13) and the second asks how they can respond to Peter's pleading (v. 37). They remain flat characters.

Note what narrative dynamics are active in the story

It is the generation of tension, predominantly through conflict and suspense, which keeps a narrative moving. Surprise and pace can also be deployed by an author and ought to be noted too. The difficulty with identifying these elements in the biblical text is that, as preachers, we are likely to know all the familiar stories so well that they do not work on us in the way that they would if we were coming to them fresh for the first time. That means we may need to work hard to realise what is actually going on in the text.

Sample sermon preparation

1. The only substantial and identifiable conflict in the story is that which is pre-existing between the disciples and the authorities. This had kept them behind locked doors in the upper room. Now, on the day of Pentecost

the events of this narrative occur right at the seat of power of those who had conspired to have Jesus removed. This irony is not lost on Peter in verse 23, 'and you, with the help of wicked men, put him to death by nailing him to the cross'. There is also a minor conflict between the man who accused the disciples of being drunk and Peter, but there is insufficient substance to develop it beyond a chronological reference.

2. There is no identifiable suspense.
3. Most of the narrative is static; the only action is condensed in the introduction and conclusion of the passage.
4. The narrative seems to depend more upon surprise than any other narrative dynamic:
    - The manner of the coming of the Holy Spirit (vv. 1–3) gives an explosive and surprising start.
    - The people gathered from many countries hearing the disciples speak in their own language is an unexpected turn (vv. 5–12).
    - The accusation that these devout men were drunk is almost comic and would certainly be out of character for them (vv. 13–16).
    - The scale of the response to Peter's preaching is an amazing surprise (v. 41).
5. Luke's deployment of pace slows the narrative down on three occasions while important motifs in the story are explained. The temptation is to pass swiftly over these slower passages. However, in verses 5–12, the commentaries see a reversal of the judgement of Babel; in verses 14–21 a biblical interpretation of the event the crowd has witnessed is given; in verses 22–36 the foundational understanding of the preached gospel is outlined. These are, therefore, highly significant sections of the narrative.

Determine who the narrator is and the narrative perspective they bring to the story
This is all about understanding the voice that is relaying the story in the text. Who are they? What is their objective?

Sample sermon preparation
1. Luke is narrating this story in the third person as he was not present during the events themselves.
2. He is writing as a Christian believer to produce an orderly account of the events for an unknown man named Theophilus. The Acts of the Apostles is a sequel to his gospel, but he clearly links the two. The basis of his writing is declared to be the fruit of eyewitness testimony and careful investigation (Lk. 1:1–4; Acts 1:1–3).
3. In his Gospel, Luke recalled that the disciples were to wait in Jerusalem until they had been, 'clothed with power from on high'. Before his ascension to heaven, at the beginning of the Acts of the Apostles, Jesus told them that when the Holy Spirit came they would receive power and would become his witnesses throughout the world (Lk. 24:49; Acts 1:8). The events of the Day of Pentecost appear to be the initial realisation of this. Therefore it could be said that Luke's objective in the narrative is to demonstrate the power of the Spirit to enable believers to act as witnesses to the gospel of Jesus Christ throughout the world.

Writing a Narrative Sermon

What am I to say?
When it comes to actually writing the sermon the most important thing to have established at the outset is what

you want to say. In narrative terms, what is your trajectory? Where do you hope to take your listeners? This means sitting down with your completed exegesis and seeking to identify this objective. For preaching to be biblical this internal direction within the sermon must be derived directly from the Bible. If it is not, then the biblical text becomes merely a pretext for the preacher to use for their own purposes.[3] It is good to attempt to express this purpose of a sermon in a single sentence. While it may not be easy, it will clarify your thinking.

Sample sermon preparation

I want those who listen to the sermon to grasp the power of the Holy Spirit to transform lives and enable us to witness effectively to the gospel of Jesus.

Who am I?

This is an important question and is determinative of the manner in which a sermon begins to be written. Inevitably, the preacher takes on the role of the narrator.

Will that narration be in the third person or the first person? In the third person, the narrator can sit more anonymously to the narrative itself.

A first-person narrator carries the immediacy of someone who has seen the events for themselves and can personally make them live for their listeners. A first-person narrative then carries a further question, which character will you be?

---

[3] Some teachers of homiletics, like Haddon Robinson, maintain that preachers should identify the 'big idea' in any given text and use that as the focus for a sermon (cf. Haddon W. Robinson, *Expository Preaching: Its Principles and Practice* or Willhite and Gibson, *Big Idea*). Others see Scripture as less determinative and would only look for a theme to be central to the narrative of a given passage.

There are a number of choices: one of the main characters in the narrative or a named individual with what might be termed 'a walk on part' and no substantive contribution to the action. Alternatively, you could put yourself even further into the background by playing the part of a bystander who was there, and saw with their own eyes, but played no part at all in the events to hand.

Sample sermon preparation
In this sermon, I decided to write a first-person narrative. Having preached this passage on numerous occasions, I felt that I wanted to explore the special edge that would be given to a sermon from someone who had witnessed for themselves, firsthand, a defining moment in the life of the Christian community.

Having made that decision, the question then was who to be. I decided to write through the eyes of Andrew. This was for three specific reasons. First, as one of the twelve Andrew was part of that first Pentecostal experience and not just an observer of it. As a preacher, I want those who listen to my sermons to be participants in the life of the Spirit, not just passive watchers of others. Secondly, as Peter's brother Andrew has both the insight and the right to talk intimately about his sibling. I felt that this would be an advantage. I also realised that it would allow me to drop a marker for the listeners to pick up who I was without actually having to be forced to tell them rather clumsily, as many do, something like, 'Hello, I'm the Apostle Andrew and today I want to tell you what happened on the very first day of Pentecost.' We need to be far more sophisticated than that and treat those who listen to our sermons with more respect. Thirdly, as Andrew has no active part in the narrative text itself it still allows the role of the narrator to be more passively in the background.

Setting

The setting of the narrative itself is determined by the biblical text. But what is the setting of the narration? Both chronologically and geographically, what is its distance from the events themselves? Further, are there matters of order, duration and frequency that need to be identified before writing the text?[4]

Sample sermon preparation

For the time and place of the narration, I chose to be at the end of the day of Pentecost looking back over the events, and musing as to their implications. This located me in Jerusalem and had the advantage of the freshness of everything that had happened still being an immediate reality for the character.

This did raise an issue of narrative order. The narration would begin after the conclusion of the events and be backward looking. I intended my closing comments to embrace 'foreshadowing' of what was to come as part of Andrew's reflections on the day. The rest of the narrative would run chronologically in parallel with the biblical text.

On matters relating to the duration of the various component parts of the biblical narrative with the narrative of my sermon, by and large I expanded the brief action pieces and contracted Peter's sermon. So, for example, verse 1 was expanded into four paragraphs while the twenty-three verses of the sermon were dealt with in seven paragraphs.

The only issue of frequency was to make two references to 'when the power came', importing the sentiment from Jesus' ascension statement in Luke 24:49. This was to reinforce the significance of the transforming power of the Holy Spirit in my stated objective for the sermon.

---

[4] See the section on order, duration and frequency in Chapter 3.

Characterisation

What can you introduce to the narrative from those things that are either directly referred to in the biblical text, or are indirectly implied that can make your characters live? Action, dialogue and sources outside the immediate text can be rich springs of insight.

Sample sermon preparation

I had two characters that I needed to bring to life, Peter and Andrew. Together they shared a common experience with the other disciples of the events of the day. On one side was the fear and anxiety that had led them to embrace the security of the upper room. To that I added a measure of claustrophobia that tempted them to leave the room to worship in the safety of the crowds at the festival.

As narrator, Andrew's story was the means by which the audience could get some insight into this experience of the Spirit and the sense of amazement and wonder that it had left with him.

Through Andrew's eyes it was also possible to view Peter as a man struggling with brokenness, disillusionment and self-loathing for having denied Jesus on the night of his arrest. Peter is then transformed by his experience of the Spirit. Andrew is full of admiration for his brother and taken with his passion, boldness and eloquence as a preacher. Yet, as only someone from your own family can, he then contrasts this with the Peter of old. The work of transforming grace is clear to see.

Narrative dynamics

In writing a narrative sermon, the preacher is not restricted to using only those devices that the biblical text uses to create and resolve tension in the given passage. As long as the sermon's content corresponds to the passage concerned, any strategy for keeping the audience involved and focused on the plot is legitimate. Drawing out conflict, creating suspense or using elements of the story to introduce surprise are means to achieve this.

Sample sermon preparation

This is a familiar passage. I was therefore concerned that it would be difficult to create any tension at all. As I discovered in the exegesis, there is little conflict and suspense to work with. Therefore, I sought to create it by setting the narrative at the end of the day. The modest level of tension this created was rooted in the audience's desire to hear through to the end what Andrew began to say at the opening of the narrative. This dynamic is then supplemented and kept alive by the elements of surprise throughout the narrative. These included the identification of Temple Mount as the location for the unfolding events and the various other revelations I had discovered about the setting. I anticipated that this would be sufficient to keep most of the audience engaged. In addition, I sought to establish a good pace throughout by editing down the slower passages in Peter's sermon that were not central to my objective.

Map the plot of the sermon

Look to have a structural template, like Lowry's Loop, that you can use to make sure that your sermon really is following a narrative form.

Sample sermon preparation

In this instance, the shape of the narrative sermon I wrote followed this pattern:

1. Upsetting the equilibrium – The setting up of the sermon as a retrospective look over the events of the last twenty-four hours. This gentle suspense is not released until the narrator's story comes to an end.

2. Analysing the discrepancy – only the evening before they were behind locked doors for fear of the authorities. A lot changed from that point in time.
3. Disclosing the clue to resolution – the experience of the coming of the Holy Spirit.
4. Experiencing the gospel – the liberation to bear witness to Jesus Christ and the forgiveness of sins.
5. Anticipating the consequences – denouement comes as the narrator reflects upon what they are going to do now with a community that has grown by three thousand and discovered a new found freedom to preach the good news of Jesus.

Delivering a Narrative Sermon

> In first-person preaching, as in comedy, delivery is critical. If you fail to present your sermon well, all the study, writing and hard work to this point will be of little value.[5]

So say Haddon and Torrey Robinson, and they are right. The closeness of the narrative style to drama becomes most obvious here. Four things need to be considered and either acted upon or dismissed.

Costumes
Would it make your character more believable to the audience (and to yourself) if you got further into character by assuming the appropriate dress and suitable props? However, if a potential costume draws attention to itself and threatens to distract from the sermon it is best to avoid it. Likewise, a character who has accompanied the People of Israel as they have journeyed through the desert to the

---

[5] Robinson and Robinson, *How You Tell It*, 60.

Promised Land will look completely out of place in a lounge suit or sports jacket and trousers.

Staging and lighting

Again, the objective is to enhance the presentation of the narrative rather than distract attention away from it.

The preacher's position

A pulpit, lectern or some other piece of church furniture which a preacher normally hides behind will not be helpful. Narrative is a far more intimate and delicate medium. However, will you stand still to speak, move around and make sympathetic movements that correlate to the story or simply sit on a bar stool and chat?[6]

The delivery itself

Narrative preaching has a different quality to that of more formal or traditional sermons. Some have observed that it is more conversational in tone, matching the inductive nature of its communication. This makes using notes particularly difficult and awkward. They can destroy the moment by causing the preacher to be less relaxed and more context-bound, rather than transporting their listeners to a distant time and place. The Robinson's, in their short book on first-person narrative, rehearse these features and then seek to make the matter abundantly clear to their readers. 'All this is to say, NO NOTES ALLOWED!!!'[7]

---

[6] Some preachers subscribe to the theory that a preacher's movements during a sermon should be carefully choreographed. For further examination of this see Reg Grant and John Reed, *Telling Stories to Touch the Heart*, 65–80 or Robinson and Robinson, *How You Tell It*, 60–1.

[7] Robinson and Robinson, *How You Tell It*, 62.

Sample sermon preparation

Costumes – my choice is not to wear first-century dress but rather to go for a very plain grey t-shirt and matching casual trousers. This corresponds with my desire for the narrator, while identified as Andrew, to actually be in the background, directing attention away from himself.

Staging and lighting – in my setup of the sermon the context for the narration was the evening of the day of Pentecost. My choice of staging and lighting is minimalist, with only a single roving spotlight in a darkened church. This recreates the sense of evening, minimises the presence of a familiar worship space and focuses the attention of the audience.

The preacher's position – under a roving spotlight, with no scripted choreography, the opportunity for movement is limited. But standing and talking to the audience, with the freedom to move around in an unexaggerated way creates the atmosphere I intend.

The delivery itself – it should be natural and conversational, without notes. Having acted a little as a teenager I found memorising scripts to be mind-numbingly tedious. Narratives, however, seem to memorise themselves for me. Not word for word, but, having looked to get the major moves of the storyline into my mind I seek to live out the events in my imagination. I picture the scenes, see the people and hear the dialogue. Then it all seems to connect inside my head and flow easily.

6

A Critique of Narrative-Style Preaching

When I first began to explore incorporating into my preaching some of the insights I had begun to discover in the narrative approach, nothing had prepared me for the response of those who listened. Some were excited and enthusiastic about what they had seen and heard. Others were deeply concerned and troubled by this new departure. This range of response has continued over the years. One pastor, having attended a day conference on narrative preaching that I had led, was gently bouncing up and down with excitement at the prospect of beginning to explore the approach himself. By contrast, a long-term friend and prayer supporter was convinced that I had fallen under the spell of a trendy technique from the United States. As far as she was concerned the sooner I gave it up and went back to preaching the gospel the better.

There is no doubt that preaching in a narrative style raises a number of significant issues for the preacher. The approach brings with it significant benefits, but not every implication is positive. Some serious and legitimate questions have been raised that need to be acknowledged and addressed.

Those who preach from an evangelical theology can find the narrative approach to be most challenging. The unique place given to the Bible as the controlling authority for

Christian life and doctrine combines with the received conviction that expository preaching is the best way for the scriptural text to be explained to the Lord's people. Narrative sermons look, feel and are very different from traditional evangelical preaching. Those from other theological and denominational traditions are less wedded to any one preaching style as being the received orthodoxy.

The main issues that the narrative preaching style raises can be broadly identified in four categories.

Cultural Issues

Perhaps the single strongest attraction of adopting a narrative style in preaching is because it is precisely the style that is now predominant in contemporary Western culture. Narrative preaching is culturally sensitive preaching. It communicates with our generation in a familiar way. The contemporary channels of communication and entertainment are loaded with stories on TV, in the movies and through the Internet. Our cultural agenda is driven forward by politicians and the media using strategically placed 'human interest' stories to explore and challenge our accepted understanding on issues of euthanasia, sexuality and embryo research. As Haddon Robinson has observed, 'We live in a story culture.'[1]

For David Hilborn, theological advisor to the Evangelical Alliance in the UK, this is the very reason why our pattern of preaching must change. Arguing for an evangelical response to postmodern culture, he points out that modernity liked to expound things – to break them down and reason them out. Such an approach has typified the churches preaching throughout the modern era.

---

[1] Robinson and Robinson, *How You Tell It*, 21.

Postmodern culture is far less wedded to such forms of communication and this therefore precipitates a crisis in which our understanding of 'the sermon' is challenged to change.[2]

Having consulted widely among evangelical leaders in the UK, Hilborn concludes that even in these circles 'the expository age' is seen as coming to an end. Derek Tidball, the Principal of London School of Theology, makes the judgement that it is now impossible to assume that a congregation will be either interested or able to handle propositional and didactic preaching. Hilborn carries a concern that if the church does not adapt its preaching it might suffer the fate of 'a maladapted dinosaur in the postmodern cultural environment.'[3] In exploring why this might be he identifies a number of potential causes in the traditional forms of expository preaching:

- *It is too rationalistic,* because postmodern people are impatient with this kind of mental discipline.
- *It is elitist,* because only intellectuals have the concentration span and linear logic to benefit from it, thus excluding 95 per cent of listeners.
- *It is too authoritarian* for the present context, with one expert giving a didactic monologue from the front.[4]

Hilborn advocates a far greater use of narrative in preaching having recognised that postmodernism is noted for a new emphasis on storytelling with writers like Douglas Coupland eloquently interpreting this new world with his

---

[2] David Hilborn, *Picking Up the Pieces: Can Evangelicals Adapt to Contemporary Culture?*, 149.
[3] Roy Clements, 'Expository Preaching in a Postmodern World', *Cambridge Papers* 7:3 (September 1998), 1.
[4] Hilborn, *Picking Up the Pieces*, 156–66.

sharp, sad tales of life in accelerated culture. Whereas in the past a story was used to illustrate a point, now the story is the point.[5] In a world that has become wary of rationalistic assertion, Hilborn believes that it may be the preferred bias of Jesus towards storytelling which needs to be recaptured to offer a constructive model of preaching for our contemporary context. He concludes:

> The problem is simply that while the classic expository model may have suited the book-driven, linear mindset of the modern West, it is hard to see how it will suit the screen-driven, multi-media mentality of postmodern culture.[6]

Such openness to change to more culturally sensitive forms of preaching has not been universally embraced on either side of the Atlantic. Attempts at being more culturally relevant are dismissed as being overly consumerist and responsible for a 'dumbing down' of the gospel with sermons which are all presentation and no content.

To adopt a contemporary style necessarily begins to integrate elements of our entertainment culture, or 'the age of show business' as Postman puts it, into our preaching. Controversy surrounded comments made by John MacArthur about the Willow Creek Community Church in this regard. He accused them of being 'ashamed of the gospel' in a book of the same name, and others have labelled them as being part of the entertainment business.[7]

While MacArthur's criticisms were not specifically aimed at the narrative preaching approach, they highlight a particular danger. There is no doubt that a style that leans

---

[5] Hilborn, *Picking Up the Pieces*, 154–5.
[6] Hilborn, *Picking Up the Pieces*, 167.
[7] Gregory Pritchard, *Willow Creek Seeker Services*, 98–9.

more towards storytelling can be much more entertaining than more traditional preaching. The temptation to 'play to the gallery' and cross the line from preacher to actor has to be resisted for both the sermon and the preacher to retain their integrity. The line between them may be difficult to discern where a congregation has enthusiastically received past attempts in the narrative style and the preacher has warmed to their subject, especially if in costume and with props and therefore taken out of themselves. Os Guinness tellingly asks what such pastors will say when the 'cows of Bashan' in Beverly Hills or the 'white-washed sepulchres' of Fortune 100 boardrooms require a prophetic word?[8] While the prophet's mantle may not rest on every preacher each week, following a more entertainment-based style does make it far easier to drift into self-indulgence, sentimentalism and gimmickry.[9]

For David Wells and Os Guinness, the quest for more culturally attuned preaching is symptomatic of a deeper and more fundamental concern. Wells believes that there is an 'anti-theological' mood presently gripping the evangelical world and changing its configuration. Reality is, as a consequence, accessed through subjective experience rather than through objective thought. The contemporary 'video culture' gives preference to intuition over reason and to feeling over truth.[10] Guinness is in agreement with Wells and holds that anti-intellectualism is 'both a scandal and a sin' because it is contrary to Jesus' first commandment to love the Lord our God with all our minds. He sees TV as being a major contributing influence in the 'dumbing down' of contemporary culture into 'idiot culture.'

---

[8] Os Guinness, *Dining with the Devil: The Megachurch Movement Flirts with Modernity*, 84.

[9] Hilborn, *Picking Up the Pieces*, 161–2.

[10] David Wells, *No Place for Truth*, 96, 181, 215.

For Guinness, television has a series of inbuilt biases that are anathema to the gospel. He believes its simplistic thought and intense emotion give TV a bias against understanding and rationality. Rapidity and variety stop viewers from engaging with the consequences of what is experienced and give the medium a bias against responsibility. The preoccupation with the present results in a bias against memory and history. While credibility is linked with plausibility, giving a bias against truth and accuracy, credibility has more to do in this context with performance than principle. He concludes that we are losing our ability to manage ideas and to think.[11] By implication, preaching that draws on these strands from contemporary culture is subject to exactly the same flaws. The principle of identification with contemporary culture is therefore viewed as a recipe for compromise and capitulation.[12]

Richard Mouw suggests that Wells and Guinness have passed too quickly over some very important issues. Judging them to have been unduly dismissive of popular religious culture he suggests 'a hermeneutic of charity' that allows a second look to be taken at things they consider not worthy of merit.[13]

While Jesus may not have been a crowd pleaser, Mouw remembers how St Augustine observed that Jesus performed miracles to get the attention of the common people. He goes on to argue that all culture is flawed, traditional and contemporary, intellectual and popular, high brow and low brow. He is concerned because contemporary popular culture can be equally easily opposed out of an uncritical

---

[11] Os Guinness, *Fit Bodies, Fat Minds: Why Evangelicals Don't Think and What to Do About It*, 10–11, 78–80.

[12] Os Guinness and John Seel (eds.), *No God but God*, 157.

[13] Richard J. Mouw, *Consulting the Faithful: What Christian Intellectuals Can Learn from Popular Religion*, 6, 13.

commitment to a traditional 'high' culture that is itself in need of Christian transformation.[14] Mouw considers this disdain for popular religious culture to be a theological defect that fails to develop an adequate theological understanding of ordinary religious people. Cardinal Newman called it 'a sort of instinct ... deep in the bosom of the mystical body of Christ.'[15]

Popular religion is the expression of men and women who bear God's image. Mouw observes that Jesus approached people in terms of the peculiarities of their context, and that the incarnation itself is a profound exercise in divine 'tailoring'. He quotes the Bishop of Edinburgh, Richard Holloway, against himself. A high churchman with little fondness for evangelicalism, Holloway wrote, 'More people go to discos than to high opera, and one of the courageous things about evangelicals is their ability to embrace bad taste for the sake of the gospel.'[16]

Mouw is particularly taken with the sentiments of Father Patrick Ryan who, commenting on the kitsch of popular Catholic devotion, shared this profound insight:

> Jesus subjected to the humiliation of bad artistic presentation pours Himself out even for those with little or no aesthetic sensibility ... How often does the Son reveal the Father in tasteless posters and plastic statues that glow in the dark? More often than I once supposed.[17]

Contemporary popular culture is not only more shaped and directed by narrative it has also become more intimate, more relational and more informal. Each of these trends,

---

[14] Mouw, *Consulting*, 59, 80.
[15] Mouw, *Consulting*, 23.
[16] Mouw, *Consulting*, 3.
[17] Mouw, *Consulting*, 5.

while the result of a number of formative influences, are either fostered or fed by TV.

Television is an intimate medium because a significant amount of programming puts the viewer in the hands of the presenter, one to one, in the viewer's own living room or bedroom. The presenter may be the viewer's guide to explain difficult situations or their mouthpiece to voice what is on their mind, in either case the relationship is an intimate one.

TV is relational on a number of levels. Some of the most popular soap operas and TV series are based around sets of relationships. *Eastenders*, *Friends* and the customers at the *Cheers* bar have a core similarity in terms of their dependence upon relationships. Indeed, part of their attraction may be on the level of providing surrogate relationships in an increasingly disconnected world.

Informality is an interesting development. Increasingly everyone is on first name terms and dress codes have changed beyond recognition. This was not so a generation ago. However, half a century of television has helped to change the world. Formality sits more easily with social distance than with friendship and intimacy.

With each of these three cultural trends a narrative style would normally score more highly than traditional preaching. It is an intimate medium because it lets the listener get empathetically inside the head of the biblical characters. It is far more conversational in style and much less preachy, also adding to the sense of intimacy. It is relational insofar as the narrative content will often open up how characters relate and interact with one another. In addition, it is more relational in presentational terms, with the more conversational approach that it forces a preacher to adopt. Greater informality is plainly obvious. This is no erudite exposition of a passage of Scripture with learned asides on the Greek and Hebrew text. Neither is it a logical argument presented with three main points, closely argued with a clearly evident structure of sub-points and illustrative material. The content of narrative preaching is normally altogether less heavy than that; it is a story.

Seeking to adapt our preaching to contemporary trends in popular culture clearly has advantages. However, it does beg a question. How many people live in this cutting-edge culture? Whatever is generally true is, after all, only generally true. For all the postmodern influences in our society there are many of us that still live according to a modernist mindset. However many people there are who are genuinely subjects of Neil Postman's 'age of entertainment', there is still a large cohort of educated individuals living in an 'age of reason'. Our culture is far from being monochrome and we must remember that.

For all our cultural diversity, however, there seems to be a universal dislike of being 'preached at'. 'Sermonising' has never been a positive term and the prevailing relativism within our culture makes it even less palatable now than it was in the past. If everyone is responsible for his or her own values and belief system, it is not the place of anyone to seek to impose them from outside. Narrative preaching works differently to the more traditional style of preaching. It tends to be inductive and implicit in its style, rather than being deductive and explicit. This leads directly into the next area to be explored, the psychological issues.

Psychological Issues

Fundamental to the narrative style of preaching is the form of reasoning that attaches to it. Normally, sermons follow a pattern of deductive reasoning in one form or another. Here the preacher begins with a biblical truth and then attempts to prove the point and argue the listener into accepting the truth. Inductive reason, by contrast, starts with questions or dilemmas and leads the listener through a process by which they can discover for themselves the answer to the dilemma. The narrative style with its initial hook and subsequent plot development is naturally inductive in its form.

Traditionally, the church has invested much in deductive forms of teaching. This has served well those who are naturally rational, logical and sequential in their thought processes and learn best by this approach. However, psychologists have also recognised that different people learn in different ways. Others are far more intuitive, holistic and visual in their thinking and are therefore far more inductively orientated in their learning. The deficiencies in the ministry of preaching on this tack are plainly obvious. A narrative-preaching style can go some way to addressing this imbalance.

Unfortunately, the inductive approach has a number of significant shortfalls. Perhaps the most significant criticism expressed against it relates to a significant loss of explicit Christian teaching in the sermon. It is not a good medium for teaching precepts and explanation of doctrine is almost impossible. Because it is an indirect medium that is less forthright than other forms of preaching, much has to be left unsaid. Indeed, it is quite possible for listeners not to get the point at all, or to even get the wrong point. Can such important biblical truths that preaching seeks to communicate be left to chance? Is it right to expect someone who listens to a narrative sermon to draw the correct conclusions? On what basis do they have the knowledge to do this? Larsen wonders whether it might not be introducing an almost Gnostic idea of salvation through knowledge.[18]

To argue that preaching in a narrative style introduces a form of neo-Gnosticism is difficult to sustain. Certainly

---

[18]   Larsen, *Old Story*, 28.

there are distinct advantages in communicating in this way. For a start, it is potentially much more memorable than a sermon with a succession of points. Few preachers will not have been met by comments after a Sunday morning service that betray the fact that one particular story, which was told as an illustration, was more powerful than the main thrust of the sermon itself. I remember one sermon I preached in Manchester in which I used what I thought was a particularly apt story about a little baby that I had spent time with during the previous week. One person after another mentioned this story over coffee afterwards, each betraying the fact in recounting the story that they really had not heard what I had been saying about it. I made a mental note at that point to be very careful in my use of baby stories in the future.

People remember good stories and they can become defining metaphors in our culture. The *Lone Ranger*, the Damascus Road experience and *Star Trek's* most famous split infinitive, 'To boldly go where no man has gone before', are illustrative of this phenomenon. We often place an individual's personal traits and behaviour against characters that have impacted our shared understanding and experience. Scrooge, Romeo, Superman, Cinderella, Uriah Heep become categories of people along with the obnoxious Alf Garnett, the morose Victor Meldrew and the cartoon creation voted the most popular TV character in the UK, Homer Simpson, with his inimitable, 'D'oh!'

Stories are more memorable also because of the way they interact with our minds. They leave pictures that endure far longer in our mind's eye than the abstract points we often make in our sermons, whatever pneumonic device we use to try and make it stick. When I was growing up we used to listen to the radio a lot as a family. There are a number of programmes that I still remember now, years later. I can picture the home of Jimmy Clitheroe, 'The Clitheroe Kid', and the bridge of HMS Troutbridge because these stories played with my imagination and left a picture there for me.

There is an academic discipline that explores how we convey ideas to one another: communication theory. One branch of this discipline deals with influencing the ideas, conviction, and actions of others: persuasion theory. Preaching falls into this category that Richard Perloff defines as:

> an activity or process in which a communicator attempts to induce a change in the belief, attitude, or behaviour of another person or group of persons through the transmission of a message in a context in which the persuadee has some degree of free choice.[19]

In the context of critiquing the narrative preaching style there are two insights that are worth noting. Speaking of advertising and advertisers, Zimbardo and Leippe observe:

> If there is one word, one concept, one process by which [they] live and die, it is 'attention'. Attract it, get it, hold it, extend it, switch it, manage it – and you are in – to first base, at least. Without it, your side is struck out. Sit down.[20]

The second is contained in *The Responsive Chord* published by Tony Schwartz in 1973. Professionals as diverse as presidential media staff and advertisers selling baby powder have deployed his ideas. He presents two competing models to explain how the media works in matters of persuasion: the 'Evoked Recall' (or 'Resonance') model and the 'Transportation' (or 'Teaching') model. He

---

[19] Richard Perloff, *The Dynamics of Persuasion*, 20.
[20] Philip G. Zimbardo and Michael R. Leippe, *The Psychology of Attitude Change and Social Influence*, 142–3.

favours the first and offers reasons why. He suggests that the best way to communicate is by evoking a response from the receiver via the set of experiences and memories that they have stored inside themselves. He observed that these experiential memories are not evoked by symbols, but rather by feelings. The best way to cue these feelings is by drama and story.[21]

The significance of these observations for the practice of narrative style preaching is clear. They indicate it to be a proven medium for effective communication of ideas that are life changing.

Biblical Issues

Is it biblical? This might seem to be a strange question to ask, but it is not an unusual one. On one level, clearly the answer is yes. When dealing with the narrative passages of the Bible a narrative sermon is obviously biblical. Yet for some, because the style is very different from the more usual form that sermons take it still begs the question. This concern is only further heightened when the loss of explicit teaching is taken into account and our biblical birthright appears to have been exchanged for a 'mess of pottage'. Is the narrative preaching style itself biblical?

Those who argue for a more deductive homiletic approach use the primacy of the *logos* (the Word) image in the opening lines of John's Gospel as foundational in signifying the profound importance of language and reason for the gospel. Further, they argue that words are precision instruments that allow the listener to distinguish truth from lies. Images and stories, on the other hand, while they

---

[21] Charles U. Larson, *Persuasion: Reception and Responsibility,* 316–22.

undoubtedly communicate powerfully on an emotional level, leave too much room for idolatrous speculation.

In addition, they draw attention to Jesus' parting instruction to the disciples in the Great Commission to engage themselves in 'teaching them to obey everything I have commanded you' (Mt. 28:18). Such an instruction would be unintelligible without the normative verbal revelation that Scripture supplies. Such an instruction requires a more deductive style for the Christian teaching ministry. Some have paralleled Paul's struggle with Gnosticism with the contemporary battle engaged with similar trends in postmodernity.[22]

While both the truth and insight of these observations can be accepted, they do not mandate a deductive style as the only appropriate preaching style. Indeed, the Bible does not mandate any particular preaching style. Scripture does not contain a new commandment ruling that 'Thou shalt always preach expository sermons'. Indeed, the deductive approach has its own roots in Greco-Roman rhetoric rather than the Bible.

The preponderance of stories in the Scriptures certainly gives biblical warrant to seeking to communicate the gospel message through narrative form. Without doubt, it can bring our preaching into closer correspondence with the text itself. While the narrative passages in the Bible are predominantly told by a narrator in the third person, like the Gospels themselves, there are a large number of examples of first-person narrative too. Nehemiah, parts of the book of Daniel and the 'we' passages from the Acts of the Apostles alongside material that can be gleaned from the Psalms and the Epistles are telling of firsthand experience. In treating the narrative portions of Scripture deductively it is a sobering question to ask whether our preaching actually does damage to the message we seek to proclaim.

---

[22] Clements, 'Expository Preaching', 2.

It seems to me that preaching in a narrative style stands up to the scrutiny of the question of whether it is biblical or not. It is biblical in both its content and style. With David Hilborn I would want to go further. Preaching in a narrative style is not an excuse for neglecting appropriate levels of preparation. While the manner and content of our preparation will, of necessity, be different, nothing should take away from its exegetic rigour. The fruit of our labour will be less on display than we might normally expect, but it should still be there. Hilborn helpfully observes that it will be more like scaffolding during sermon construction than a framework for delivery.[23]

Issues for the Preacher and Congregation

When I was first introduced to narrative preaching I was excited to have discovered a new way of handling and presenting the Scriptures. Having preached most weeks for almost two decades this was a refreshing addition to my preaching repertoire. Yet it remains a demanding homiletic discipline. It requires both creativity and a sensitive touch. It is easy to fail to make the point that you are driving at, or conversely, to make it too heavily, so that the narrative medium is itself destroyed. In an early attempt at a narrative sermon I was so anxious to make sure my listeners understood what the main character was feeling that I mentioned it three or four times during the sermon itself. I was careful in each instance to change the words so that it would not seem repetitious, yet, on listening to a tape afterwards that was exactly how it did seem. I had been far too clumsy with a very delicate medium. I learned that the rules that normally relate to good preaching in a more traditional

---

[23] Hilborn, *Picking Up the Pieces*, 160.

sermon morph in strange ways when a sermon follows a narrative pattern.

How a sermon is concluded is another case in point. Do you leave the listeners to draw their own conclusions or do you use the opportunity at the end of the sermon to do some application? Fred Craddock maintains that we have names for those who insult us by explaining a joke as they tell it again. He advocates allowing listeners to draw their own conclusions from what a preacher has said.[24] While this would be my own preference, some practitioners do seek sensitively to make a gentle application at the end a narrative sermon. Having completed the content of the sermon they pause, wait a few seconds, and come back into their own character and in a few sentences underline the controlling idea that has driven the narrative that they have been preaching.

Having long resisted this approach, I have to acknowledge that a number of preachers known to me have spoken positively of how effective a strategy it can be. However, that does not diminish how delicate the medium of narrative is and how carefully such application should be planned so as not to undermine the whole endeavour.

Stories have a universal appeal that makes narrative a particularly good medium to adopt in a mixed age context. The first time I preached the 'Breaking the Sound Barrier' sermon based on Acts 4:1–31 in Chapter 7 was in such a context. It was a church weekend away and I was the visiting speaker. The weekend was following the theme of prayer and, while the young people had their own programme for most of the time away, one session was planned to bring both streams together. It was amazing to see the children sitting quietly entranced by the presentation

---

[24] Fred Craddock, *As One Without Authority: Essays on Inductive Preaching*, 62.

of the Bible story. It was then used as a springboard into group activities that included praying together and it worked far better than I had dared to hope.

Of course, a particular challenge with narrative sermons for a preacher is how to maintain surprise in the plot of the sermon when a congregation knows how the story ends up. Whichever way you tell it, David kills Goliath with a pebble from his sling, Daniel escapes from both the lion's den and the fiery furnace, and the Samaritan in Jesus' parable ends up being the good guy. With the hard work of application completed and the imagination engaged the preacher must ask the spiritually discerned question, 'Where do I take this?' Good stories bear retelling. If not, there would be no place for a theatre to put on a play of Shakespeare or Ibsen. Indeed, the video and DVD market is driven by the desire of people to hear the same story again.

The most powerful attraction of narrative preaching for a congregation is that it speaks of life. Every Sunday worshippers arrive at church with a whole array of concerns. Pressures at work, broken relationships, and seemingly irresolvable moral dilemmas combine with the minor hurts and frustrations of everyday life and sit just below the surface of the seemingly carefree worshipper. Narrative meets these worshippers where they are as they seek to wrestle with how to live Christianly in their own circumstances. Good stories tell life truths that are universal and can speak into the smaller particular truths of our lives. Calvin Miller is convinced that as preachers, 'We are the story makers, the makers of hope, the makers of irreducible meaning.'[25]

Well told stories also have the ability to cause a listener to reserve or suspend their judgement in a way that more traditional preaching does not. Because the style is less

---

[25] Calvin Miller, *Spirit, Word, and Story: A Philosophy of Marketplace Preaching*, 161–9.

confrontational the listener wants to see how the story ends. This greater openness means that there is far more opportunity for the underlying message of the gospel to be given a fair hearing, rather than just to bounce off our intellectual defences. Fred Craddock describes how this works in the following terms:

> A narrative is told with distance and sustains it in that the story unfolds on its own, seemingly only casually aware of the hearer, and yet all the while the narrative is inviting and beckoning the listener to participation in its anticipation, struggle, and resolution.[26]

Stories reflect life and, therefore, there is an immediate connection with the listener. The movie industry talks about the 'emotional truth' of a film when they refer to its broad message. With their various production techniques and the performances of the actors the film seeks to touch both the minds and hearts of the audience. This is the power of the movies and what makes a feature presentation into a full-blooded experience rather than just entertainment. With the Roman General, Maximus Decimus Meridius, in the movie *Gladiator* you feel the loss of his wife and family and the need for revenge that drives him. In the acclaimed British film *Secrets and Lies*, the crippling effect of untold stories on the relationships of one family is painful to witness.

A well-told narrative sermon has the same impact. Haddon and Torrey Robinson point out how this enables the listeners to a sermon to not only hear God's truth, but to experience it too.[27] The only limitations on the medium are

---

[26] Fred Craddock, *Overhearing the Gospel*, 123.
[27] Robinson and Robinson, *How You Tell It*, 21.

the limits of the imagination of the preacher and listener to get inside the story and understand.

Of course, ultimately the novelty of a new style of preaching will wear off for both preacher and congregation. But beneath the initial interest that is generated by something new is a means of communication for the preacher to deploy that is effective in its own right and genuinely appropriate to the present cultural context in which we find ourselves.

Part 3

Narrative Sermons

This section of the book contains sample sermons of the three different styles of narrative sermon that were outlined in chapter four. With the exception of the second sermon in Chapter 8 on David and Abigail, which was written by Paul Borden, all the others are mine. They are raw transcripts that have not been honed for publication. Indeed, I have even resisted the temptation to update them according to what I learnt having preached them.

I have also purposefully omitted a commentary upon them to enable you to interact with them for what they are. However, let me give you a few guidelines as to how you might do that:

1. Begin by reading the sermon. It is best to read it out loud as they were all written for the ear rather than the eye. Indeed, if you can get someone to read it for you it will be even better as that will enable you to experience the sermon as if you were a member of an audience.
2. Spend some time thinking about what you have listened to before you begin to analyse it.
   - What worked and why? For example, what was particularly evocative and memorable? What seemed hackneyed, forced or false?
   - If narrative works by a process of induction, what was the journey that the sermon took you on? What issues did it lead you to interact with? Where did it leave you?
   - Is it possible to try and sum up the writer's underlying intention in writing the sermon in this way? What was the writer trying to communicate?
3. Having interacted with the oral presentation of the sermon return to the text and look at its structures. Is it possible to identify how it has been constructed? What are the major moves and how effective were they?

Enjoy!

7

When the Preacher is the Narrator of the Story
(Third-Person Narrative Sermons)

Paralysed by Fear: 1 Samuel 9:1 – 10:27

He was crouching as low as he could get. He could even smell the dirt his nose was so close to the ground. There were plenty of bags among which to hide, but he felt so exposed and vulnerable. So he clung closer and closer to the ground because he really didn't want to be seen. His heart was pounding and he thought that if it didn't stop beating so loud, people would discover him just through the noise it was making. Every time someone passed by he held his breath and broke out in a cold sweat. What he feared most was happening, and he seemed powerless to stop it; it was all out of control. There were noises again and this time they were not moving past. They were systematically going through all the baggage that people had brought with them, he knew that it was impossible to escape, so he just crouched lower and lower with his face to the ground. But that wasn't easy because he was a tall man and his legs were beginning to cramp and the pain was excruciating. It was only a matter of time before they tipped over the bags that were surrounding him and discovered his pitiable figure, but what else could he do? He redoubled his attempts to become one with the earth and so avoid the inevitable.

It had all begun not long before when Saul was at home in Benjamin with his family, and his father, Kish, had sent him out with a servant to find his donkeys which had gone missing. Now that was a thankless task, they could have been anywhere. You know what donkeys are like; they've got minds of their own. Well, Saul and the servant set out and immediately began to draw blanks. They passed through the hill country of Ephraim, and there was no sign of the donkeys. They searched the area around Shalisha, and still no donkeys! Next they went into the district of Shaalim, and you guessed it, still no donkeys. Finally having passed through the territory of Benjamin and finding not a trace of those blessed donkeys, even in the district of Zuph, Saul was ready to give up; after all it had been three whole days.

It was at this point that the servant had a brainwave. Living in these parts was a man of God, a seer, who had an awesome reputation. He was highly respected by everyone and everything he said came true. He had the gift of putting his finger on things, so perhaps he might be able to tell them where the donkeys were. Saul warmed to the idea, so off they went.

Well, as fate should have it, as they walked into the town who should be coming towards them but Samuel himself; only, they didn't know that it was Samuel.

Now, the night before the Lord had revealed to Samuel that on the following day he was going to send him a man from Benjamin to anoint as leader of Israel. One who would deliver the Lord's people from the Philistines: 'I have looked on my people, for their cry has reached me.' God had told him. Now, as Samuel was walking down the street the Lord spoke to him again, 'This is the man I spoke to you about who will govern my people.'

Saul approached Samuel and asked him where the seer's house was. A big grin spread over Samuel's face. 'I am the seer,' he said, 'come with me because I want us to eat together today. Then tomorrow, I will tell you all that is in your heart. And don't worry about those donkeys that you lost three days ago, they've been found. Indeed, what really matters is that the desire of all Israel is turned towards you and your father's family.'

Saul was a wee bit concerned about all of this. It was sounding a touch spooky. Now, they had gone to the seer to find out about the donkeys, but he hadn't really put much store by it. After all he had never heard of the man, it was the servant's suggestion. Then all this 'desire of all Israel' stuff, where was that leading? The last thing he wanted to do was get drawn in to some heavy religious scene, who knew where that might lead. So, he played his best card, 'You must be mistaken,' he said, 'I'm actually from Benjamin, you know the smallest tribe of Israel, with the least reputation, and, well, my clan is the least of all the clans of Benjamin, so I think that you're probably just mistaken!' However, by the time Saul got it all out Samuel was striding off and Saul was left with his servant wondering what they were getting into. He felt his stomach begin to tighten with a sense of foreboding, but he persuaded himself that there was no harm in staying for the meal and taking advantage of the offer of lodging, so they set off after him.

When Saul and his servant sat down for the meal the most incredible smells and aromas confronted them, and when the seer told the cook to bring the piece of meat that had been laid aside, and a full leg with all the trimmings was put before him, Saul's taste buds were truly set alight. Now this was all well and good, but where was the catch? He was really getting quite concerned because the more time he spent with Samuel, the weirder it all became.

After the meal, Samuel took them home and they went up on the roof. It was a warm, barmy evening, and after the heat of the room in which they had eaten it was the most comfortable place to be. He and Samuel talked for ages, and his fears from earlier in the evening began to disappear. When finally Samuel left him, Saul chose to sleep in the relative coolness that the roof provided, and rest came easy. The donkeys were found, he'd had a good meal and Samuel didn't **appear to be the deranged religious fanatic that he had feared he might be. He slept soundly.**

The next morning Samuel was the consummate host, and, as they walked together to the edge of town, the seer suggested to Saul that he send his servant on ahead because he had a message from God for him. It was like a lead weight had dropped right down to his bowels. He couldn't think, his mind had seized up and he could feel the beads of perspiration forming on his forehead and the back of his hands and neck. But there was nothing he could do; he could only accede to the request. But this was what he had feared most. This was the catch. Now he was going to have to pay for that meal and the hospitality, and who knew what this seer character was up to?

When the servant was a safe distance ahead of them Samuel took out a flask of oil and poured it over Saul's head and kissed him. Saul didn't know what to do. It was running down his back, in his eyes, he opened his mouth to speak and he got a mouthful. It was all over his coat and it was sticky and messy and all he could think of was that he was going to have to travel all the way home like this. What was this idiot up to?

With the oil trickling into his ears it was difficult to make out exactly what Samuel was saying, but it was something about the Lord making him, Saul, leader over his inheritance, whatever that meant! Then it began to dawn on him, Samuel was talking about the kingship. It was all the rage throughout Benjamin. The Philistines were on the march again and informed opinion had it that Israel needed a king, like the other nations. But what was this seer thinking of, the very thought was laughable. Think about it, he couldn't even find a bunch of lost donkeys! He would have laughed, but the thought died as his stomach tied itself neatly in another knot. Samuel was serious, and what was more he was now doing some predicting.

'When you get to Rachel's tomb at Zelzah two men will meet you and tell you that the donkeys have been found and your father is now worried about you. Then when you reach the great tree at Tabor you will meet three men going up to God at Bethel. One will be carrying three young goats; one will be carrying three loaves of bread; and another will be carrying a full skin of wine. They will greet you and offer you two loaves of bread which you will accept.' Saul could hardly take it in, but the seer hadn't finished yet. He had now moved on to Gibeah of God, where the Philistine outpost was. Saul knew that place well because Gibeah was home. But what Samuel was saying just served to intensify the sense of dread that he was feeling. He was going to meet a procession of prophets coming down from the high place in full flow with their lyres and tambourines and flutes and harps, prophesying for all they are worth. When the Spirit of the Lord came on these men there was no telling what they might do, they were in a kind of trance, with the rhythmic music and their spiritual ecstasies. It was the last thing that Saul wanted to be or do. Everyone looked at them as though they were odd. They were religious nutcases, everyone knew that. 'You will be changed', Samuel was saying, 'changed into a different person.' That was just it, Saul didn't want to be changed into a different person, it scared him, and it frightened him.

'Once these signs are fulfilled, do whatever your hand finds to do, for God is with you.' Saul didn't know what to say. His mind was whirling round and round, his insides were churning, it was panic, blind panic, fuelled by raging fear, he just knew he had to get away. Then he could put it all out of his mind, yes that's what he'd do.

But, it was as he turned to leave that it began to happen. How do you put it into words, it was as though God just reached in and touched him on the inside, something changed, the sense of foreboding dissolved away and the fear disappeared. As he walked along, seeking to catch up his servant, it was as if the world were a better place. What Samuel had been talking about didn't seem so daunting now. He felt like a new man, transformed, ready to face anything. When the first prophesy was fulfilled at Zelzah, and then the second at Tabor, Saul began to get excited. God really was doing something with him, he could hardly believe it, but it was true, he was walking on air. But things were to change. Until this point, he hadn't given much thought to what was coming next. The sense of what God had done within him and the exhilaration of the seer's fulfilled predictions had just carried him along. But, as Tabor faded into the distance, Saul began to think about what was coming next. The thought didn't fill him with the same sense of excitement. The prophets were an odd bunch. People looked at them in a derisory way, especially when the Spirit came upon them, and Samuel had said that the Spirit of the Lord would come upon him in power. That sounded frightening, and to make it worse, this was going to happen at Gibeah to, at home. The sense of dread began to return, and when, in the distance, he caught the sound of their procession and prophesying carrying on the wind, his anxiety level began to heighten, and as they came up over the crest of the hill it was too late. The Spirit came upon Saul and he began to dance and move with the beat and rhythm of their music. Then came the prophesying, it was as though he had done it all his life. The words just flowed and all sense of time departed. The music and the words, and the words and the music just went on and on.

How long it lasted the Lord alone knows, but Saul was exhausted, and as he drew near to his home he caught people looking at him and whispering. At times he thought he heard what they were saying, 'Is it true, has Saul become one of those prophets now?' He felt incredibly self-conscious. What had he done when the Spirit was upon him? What were people saying about him, more to the point, what were they thinking about him? As he thought about it he got more and more worked up. This was not good, added to which, the very thought of being king scared him witless. All of those things that he had been suspicious of from when he first met Samuel began to build up within him and Saul just couldn't cope any more. This was just too much to handle, so he decided there and then to shut it out of his mind.

When he got home with his servant he was met by his uncle, and the question was the familiar one, 'Where have you been?' That was a daft question, 'Looking for those donkeys,' he replied, 'and when we got to Zuph and still couldn't find them, we went to see Samuel.' His uncle's ears pricked up at the sound of Samuel's name, 'What did he have to say to you?' he asked. At this point Saul's heart was thumping, he almost let it all out and told the whole story of what the Lord was doing in his life, how God had touched his heart; the men at Zelzah; the incident at Tabor; and the prophesying bit when he arrived at Gibeah, but he thought better of it. What would his uncle think? What would he tell his father? In that instant he decided not to say anything about the kingship and what God had been doing in his life, 'Oh,' he said, 'he assured us that the donkeys had been found, so we came home.'

Now it was some time later that Samuel called the whole of Israel together at Mizpah. There were tens of thousands of people there by the time Kish and his family arrived. They deposited their baggage with those who had been charged **to keep an eye on it** and it was some baggage pile too. Can you imagine how many bags that number of people bring to a gathering like that?

Well, when everyone had arrived and Samuel gathered them together the reason for this extraordinary assembly became clear. Samuel began by recounting how that Lord, the God of Israel had led their ancestors out of Egypt, he talked about the wilderness wanderings, the law, and all the victories that the Lord had given to them, and Saul wasn't really listening. He had heard all this before and his mind was wandering. He was back at that evening and his own personal encounter with Samuel, and how he had been **anticipant of the angle the seer** was coming from. Well, that had died a death. Nothing had come of it and Saul had begun to conclude that the man of God had just been mistaken this time. It was as he was playing with this comforting thought that Saul was brought back to reality with a jolt. Samuel's eyes were blazing as he told the people that they had rejected the Lord who had delivered them from their calamities and distresses by their constant requests for a king.

Saul broke out in a cold sweat; he had to get out of there. If Samuel spotted him it was all over, but perhaps if he made himself scarce, the lot would fall to someone else. As the people stood riveted to Samuel's oration, Saul quietly made his way out of the crowd. But where could he go? For a while, as he discreetly edged his way past people he had no idea, but then the thought struck him, no one would find him in the baggage pile, so that was where he headed.

From his hiding place right in the centre of the pile, he could just make out what was going on. The tribes were being called before Samuel one at a time. He caught the names of Naphtali, Issachar, Judah – it was a process of elimination – Reuben, and Gad, and Zebulan. He knew that it was going to end up with Benjamin. He felt his muscles tighten; he wanted to run away as fast as he could, but he resisted the urge and remained hidden. Then it was the clans of Benjamin, he knew it, as soon as they started he knew it, Matri's clan would be chosen. Then it was his name, his name, they had chosen him, even though he wasn't there! What happened next, he didn't know. He was just glad that they wouldn't know where he was.

Suddenly he felt exposed, there were people in among the baggage, and they were turning the bags over. How did they know where he was? He had been so careful when he slipped away. Even those guarding the bags hadn't seen him, or so he thought. However, they were making a systematic search and they were getting closer and closer. And the closer they got the nearer he crouched to the dirt, he could even smell it. But it wasn't easy because he was a tall **man, and the cramp was beginning to claim his calves, he** longed to relieve the pressure but they were getting closer as the bags tumbled over to his left and his right. He managed to inch his way a little lower, but that only served to increase the cramp to an excruciating level. He could even taste the dirt he was so close to the ground. He couldn't get any lower, and the bags that were toppling over were getting closer and closer. There was no way out, a sense of nausea completely enveloped him. This was it as the bags around him tumbled away and he was left, exposed, humiliated in his fear. The one chosen to be king, cowering, frightened and scared.

As they lifted him up, dusted him down and began to lead him off towards Samuel, he wanted to say something, to explain, to find an excuse, but nothing came. He was paralysed with fear and there was nothing that he could do about it. He felt so helpless, and yet he stood head and shoulder above the men who had found him, and Samuel was quick to draw attention to it. 'Do you see the man the

Lord has chosen?' he said, 'There is no one like him in all of Israel.'

Saul was still struck dumb, and the people were acclaiming him, 'Long live the king! Long live the king!' Saul wanted the earth to open and swallow him, 'Long live the king!' they shouted. He wanted to be alone with his servant looking for the donkeys. 'Long live the king!' went the refrain. His wished for none of this to ever have happened, but the people just kept right along, 'Long live the king! Long live the king!' There was a mood of celebration about. The Lord had answered their prayers, and given them a king, one who even looked like a king, a fine stature of a man. But inside Saul felt little, he felt humiliated, he felt totally incapable and inadequate.

When Samuel sent everyone home, Saul found himself escorted by his very own detachment of the 'valiant men'. He felt such a fraud as they accompanied him back to Gibeah. They were real men, men of courage, men of character, men to look up to. Beside them he was a fake. Now the people had taken to bringing him gifts to pledge their loyalty to his reign, a kind of coronation gift. One bunch of troublemakers refused. Instead, they mocked Saul to his face, 'What use is this man? How is he going to save us from the Philistines?' It was as though they had seen directly into Saul's soul and knew what he was really like. He felt he ought to say something, to tell them that he was God's chosen one, to tell them of the miraculous signs that Samuel had predicted which had come true. He felt he ought to slay them with words and make them buckle down under his newly found authority as king, but the words wouldn't come. It was just the same as when he chose not to share with his uncle all the things that God was doing in his life. He was afraid of what his uncle would have thought then, and he was afraid of what people would think now. The 'valiant men' thought that he acted with marvellous restraint, treating these troublemakers with the contempt they deserved, but Saul knew better, he was still hiding in the baggage.

Breaking the Sound Barrier: Acts 4:1–31

It was difficult to see them because there were so many people standing there listening to them speak. But, if you listened hard from the back of the crowd you could still hear, and with the warmth of the evening sun on your face and the birds singing, ah!

Then, suddenly, without any warning there was pushing and shoving and the crowd's attention was distracted. People began to protest, 'Who do you think you are? What do you think you're …,' but the guards were well built and when people realised who it was; they just moved out of the way for them.

Behind them, all dressed up with their splendid robes flowing in the breeze were the Sadducees. These leaders of the people, these moneyed families who ruled the nation and the temple in their own interest, they were obviously wound up by the speakers who had been telling stories about Jesus. They had been saying that this man who they had lobbied to be executed by the Roman authorities had been raised from the dead by God. Actually thousands of people had decided to follow Jesus since he had been crucified by the occupying army. The authorities were worried that it was getting out of hand.

Well, they just made their way through the crowd and arrested them. Just there and then. Right there in front of everyone and no one did a thing. Well, what could they do? Lift a finger to help and you'd be in exactly the same boat, arrested and thrown in jail.

Prison isn't the most comfortable place to spend the night. Jerusalem nights can get chilly and a dirty, drafty floor doesn't guarantee a good **night's** sleep. So when Peter and John were hauled before a kangaroo court the next morning they were already feeling the worse for wear. Dirty, smelly and tired they felt at a distinct disadvantage as they were paraded before the members of the High Priest's family. Annas the High Priest was there as was **Caiaphas**, John, Alexander and a group of others who they didn't recognise. But they were so obviously a part of the 'powers that be' just by the self-important way they acted. Then it dawned on him, this was the Sanhedrin – the most powerful council in the country. Peter was nervous. What did they want? What were they going to do with him and John? He could feel his knees begin to tremble and his stomach was churning.

'By what power or what name did you do this?' No one had told them why they had been arrested, but Peter had spotted a face he recognised from the day before off to one side. It was not a face he was going to forget. The crippled beggar from the Temple Gate was someone everyone knew because they passed by him and his begging bowl every time they went into the Temple to worship. The day before he had asked Peter and John for money but they had been unable to respond. Instead, they had prayed with him – and this man who had been crippled from birth – just got up and walked. Now everybody knew him and knew that this wasn't some sleight of hand by a group of religious hucksters. No one could believe their eyes and word had spread like wildfire. That had been why there was such a crowd around them when the guards had come to arrest them.

Suddenly, Peter felt a surge of power travel through him. It started in his heart. It travelled downwards and his legs stopped trembling and upwards and spilled out of his mouth.

'If it's about the kindness we did to a cripple yesterday, then hear this, it is by the name of Jesus Christ of Nazareth.

You remember, the one you had crucified by the Romans. Well, the grave couldn't hold him because God raised him from the dead. It is because of Jesus that this man stands before you healed today. Forty years he was crippled, and Jesus healed him.'

With that Peter pointed at the man, and they all knew him; they had passed him every day too. Sometimes throwing a coin into his begging bowl and feeling somehow better for it afterwards!

Peter was in full flood now, and surprised himself by the words that were flowing from his lips. 'Don't you remember in the Psalms that it says that the stone that was rejected would become the most important cornerstone? There is no way under heaven to get to God or find salvation but by Jesus.'

The stiffness in his back from a night spent on the prison floor that had previously caused him to be a little hunched up had disappeared. He wasn't intimidated by their presence anymore either, they could see that. His courage and the power of his words were obvious too, though it was plainly evident that he had never gone to school.

They had Peter and John removed to another place and went into closed session. What were they going to do? They needed to have them gagged so that they wouldn't disrupt the Temple any more with this teaching about a dead Messiah who had come back to life. Yet everyone living in Jerusalem was coming to the Temple to worship and praise God because an outstanding miracle had taken place with the crippled beggar.

Peter and John were brought back in and summarily banned from talking about Jesus. Peter was already there with an answer. 'Tell me, what should I do, obey you or obey God! There's no way that I can stop telling about what I know!' Even Peter was a little surprised to hear the words coming out of his mouth. Well, they issued some more threats against them and then let them go. As Peter and John walked into the daylight as free men the mixture of fear and tension of the last day just slipped away. They wanted to jump up and down and shout 'hallelujah!' at the top of their voices.

That night all the followers of Jesus were together for a meeting. There is something important in coming together. For a start you know that you're not alone, no matter what might happen. You could have heard a pin drop as everyone listened to what had happened to Peter and John. When they finished telling the story someone began to say a Psalm:

'Sovereign Lord you made the heaven, and the earth and the sea, and everything in them.' By the time they reached the end of the first line everyone had joined in. God created the world; God ruled the world; if God was for them, who could be against them?

Someone else was praying, 'Lord Herod and Pontius Pilot tried to kill your message off by their conspiracy against Jesus. But you turned their evil into good and the defeat of the cross into the victory of the resurrection.'

'Amens!' echoed round the room as people murmured their agreement.

Another voice took up the theme, 'Now they're threatening us, now they're trying to stop us. Lord help us to speak your word with great boldness like Peter. Lord, stretch out your hand to heal and perform miracles and signs and wonders through the holy name of Jesus.'

Everyone was taken up into the prayers. The Holy Spirit filled the meeting and the same sense of boldness began to throb in their hearts just as it had in Peter's as he spoke to the High Priest and the Sanhedrin. In that moment they knew that there was nothing that they couldn't face if God was with them. As the Holy Spirit poured God's strength into their hearts and minds and spirits as they prayed – they rejoiced that they could speak freely with God together, and that in response the very gates of heaven were opened to them.

At that moment the place where they were meeting shook as God himself said, 'AMEN!' And the result was awesome. In the face of the threats and the growing hostility of the officials of state, the whole church experienced the same boldness as the great apostle Peter. The sound barrier between earth and heaven had been broken, with startling results.

Guess Who is Coming to Dinner: Luke 7:36–40

Have you had one of those days or been in one of those situations where everything has just begun to go wrong. You've been expecting something pleasant and it turns out to be an utter nightmare. You have been looking forward to it in anticipation, and yet it has left you thoroughly uncomfortable by the experience. Well, if you've ever had something like that happen to you, you won't find it difficult to get inside of the experience of one of the characters in this morning's story.

You see the situation in which Simon found himself was exactly that. He was a religious man, a spiritual man. His belief was sincere, he meant business with God and he wanted to learn. He was keen to understand all he could and was open to learn, even if the truth came from the most unusual of sources. That was why he had invited Jesus to dinner.

Now he was a Pharisee, but an open-minded one who was not afraid to think outside of the box, unlike some of his colleagues. Being a good Jew he attended synagogue. But this was more than a mere formality of weekly religious obligation. He was committed to spending time in Bible study, seeking to make connections between what the Scriptures said and his life and how he lived it.

So when the opportunity presents itself to invite Jesus to dinner he grasps it with both hands. It's an opportunity that excites him. Jesus had been causing a bit of a stir and many people were following him; his wisdom was renowned. Simon himself had not yet made up his mind, but at a dinner party, he would have the opportunity to listen to Jesus for himself and draw his own conclusions.

Well, with all of that expectation and looking forward, the evening of the meal arrives. The table is set; it's quite low down, just a few inches off the ground, in fact. The guests at the meal are reclining on small couches, again just a few inches off the ground. Leaning on their left hand with their head by the table, their right hand is free to eat with. Their feet are pointing away from the table. That is important, as we shall see.

Now it was common practice when you had a Rabbi round for a meal, especially one who was good to listen to, to have a kind of semi-open house. In this way people could come and stand in the shadows or the doorway to listen to what the teacher had to say.

Well, this is what happened on this particular night. The guests had come and were reclining at the table. Others had arrived and were lining the room listening to the conversation between Simon, his friends and Jesus.

To begin with Simon was pleased by those who had turned out; they were good people, respectable people. The evening promised to be a success. But then, who should slip in but one of the prostitutes from the town. What do you do with gatecrashers? In that spiritual company she stuck out like a sore thumb. She did not fit at all, and as Simon sat at the table trying to listen to Jesus, his attention was focusing on this prostitute, this whore. She was a notorious sinner. Her sin was obvious, and, like dirt, it could easily rub off on those who were present and leave the whole occasion tainted. Just the thought of who she was, and what she did, revolted Simon; more than that, as the host, he became more and more aware of how awkward everybody else felt at her presence. He didn't want her there and they didn't want her there.

Well, actually, they perhaps did want her there, because he spied them out of the corner of their eyes looking at her anyway, after all it wasn't as though she was unattractive, quite the opposite, she was really rather pretty. And with all this lofty theological conversation going on, there were many eyes that were beginning to wander. And, if it wasn't the eyes, it was the nose because these women had a smell, **not an unpleasant aroma, but rather an alluring, arousing** smell.

Simon did not want her there. He hadn't bargained for this sort of distraction and did not relish having to deal with it. He found it impossible to express his disapproval and so the pressure increasingly built up inside him.

She was standing so close to Jesus yet it seemed to have no effect on him or his participation in the conversation. Well, if that wasn't bad enough, things went from bad to worse as the meal continued. She continued to hover around Jesus' feet, slightly away from the table. And then, well, she was overcome by some kind of emotion and she fell to her knees weeping, only to realise that as she wept, her tears were fall-ing on his feet, and, seeing no towel to hand, she unfastened her hair and wiped his feet with it! Have you ever heard of such a thing? It was scandalous for any Jewish woman not to have her hair tightly done up on her head, and here is this whore using her hair in such a way with a Rabbi.

And then, as if things couldn't get worse, finding herself in such an intimate proximity to his feet, what does she do? With some kind of affectionate gratitude, she starts to smother his feet with kisses, and, if that is not enough, the perfume that she was wearing when she came in ... well, there's another bottle of it round her neck, and she takes the top off and pours that all over his feet too, so that the whole room reeks of a whore house! Imagine what it looked like! Can you begin to comprehend Simon's reaction? It was so unseemly, so sensual, so inappropriate. Oh, he could imagine what the talk was going to be for months. 'Prostitute gets intimate with preacher at rabbinical dinner', kind of stories. Jesus, however, was not moved – no impatience, no embarrassment: actually, he didn't seem bothered at all. Not bothered by who she was or what she was doing. Indeed, Jesus seemed altogether more upset with Simon's obvious agitation. Simon, you see, was beginning to draw some conclusions about Jesus. If he really was a holy man, well, he wouldn't stand for this, would he? If he really was a prophet he would know what kind of common hooker this woman was, if he was … well, surely he would put a stop to it, wouldn't he?

Well as this stuff is flying around inside Simon's head, Jesus makes his move. 'Simon, I have something to tell you'. You could have heard a pin drop. Everybody knew what was going on, and this is obviously the critical moment when it's all going to spill out into the open. Everybody was aware, in that discreetly polite way, but aware all the same; sensitive, perhaps even sympathetic to poor old Simon's position, and his dilemma, glad it was happening in his house and not theirs. Now Jesus was going to say something, this so-called religious teacher who had allowed a prostitute to caress his feet in public, what was he going to say? This supposed spiritual leader, gloriously unaware of the difficult position he had placed his host in. What was he likely to come out with? Some considered him a holy man, but his holiness was revealed to be stained with the morals of the gutter. Yet everyone wanted to hang on his words. They could dine out on this story for years to come.

But Jesus tells a story. 'There were these two men who owed money to a money changer. One owed 500 denarii, one owed 50,' (a denari was roughly a farm worker's daily wage – not a great amount to those sitting round the table, but not insubstantial). 'Well, these two men,' says Jesus 'couldn't pay their debts. So, do you know what, the money changer forgave the debt; he let it pass and let them off. Which of those two do you think would love the money changer more, Simon?'

The answer was so obvious and yet Simon had one of those ominous feelings. Jesus was leading him down a path, but he couldn't see where it was going. The answer was out there, but, at this particular moment in time, he had not got a handle on it. His mind went into overdrive. He knew that this whole situation was going to be turned on him but there was absolutely nothing he could do about it. He couldn't get an angle on what Jesus was going to say, and so, rather pathetically, he says 'Well, er, I suppose the one who had the bigger debt cancelled.'

'You judge correctly,' says Jesus.

'You see this woman,' he says, looking at the woman, and speaking to Simon.

Talk about a stupid question! Simon has seen nothing but that prostitute since the minute that she walked into the room. 'You see this woman,' says Jesus and then begins to compare that woman with Simon.

'You didn't give me any water to wash my feet, but she has wet them with her tears and dried them with her hair'. Simon begins to think, I haven't done anything wrong. If you have a friend round, you wash their feet when they arrive but not an ordinary guest!

'You didn't greet me with a kiss,' says Jesus, 'but this woman has not stopped kissing my feet since she arrived.' Again Simon thinks, but you're a guest not a friend. I've been courteous, I've been civil, and then the penny begins to drop. He's calling this prostitute a woman! He hadn't seen a woman at all. All he had seen was the prostitute.

'You didn't anoint my head with oil,' said Jesus, 'but she has anointed my feet with perfume.' Everything in Simon resented what Jesus was saying and he regretted inviting him at all. What had he done to deserve such abuse? This evening was supposed to be a time of elevated spiritual conversation, but it had now been irretrievably spoiled by this whore's antics.

But Jesus hadn't finished, he was still speaking, 'She loves much. Therefore Simon, she must have been forgiven much. The one who loves little, well, they have been forgiven little.' The implication was clear. He, Simon, a Pharisee, had been forgiven little. Well, what was there to forgive? He'd studied the Bible, he'd kept the Law and he'd tried to live a good life. If forgiveness was what it was all about, then bad people obviously had a head start and that just wasn't fair.

Simon had wanted to be genuinely open to learn something from Jesus, he had wanted to get at the spiritual truth, he wanted some stimulating God talk, but Jesus had taken a wholly different line. Simon had a rude awakening that particular night. Having Jesus to dinner was a wholly uncomfortable experience, because he opened up some home truths for his host.

Leaving Simon wrestling with the indignation generated by his pride and self righteousness, Jesus turns to the woman and says, 'Woman, your sins are forgiven, your faith has saved you. Go in peace.' The other guests sit there dumbstruck. Who is this who even forgives sins?

And that's where the story breaks off at just the most frustrating point. What are you going to do, Simon? The thought is there. Are you going to recognise your need for forgiveness? Or are you going to stand aloof, your sensibilities injured by Jesus' thoughtlessness?

8

When the Preacher is a Character in the Story (First-Person Narrative Sermons)

You'll Never Believe This!: Acts 2:1–41

I don't know what to say! How can I even start to describe the last twenty-four hours to you? Unexpected, well it certainly took us by surprise. We thought something was going to happen, but not like this, nothing like this. You could call it amazing because it was certainly that, awe-inspiring, miraculous even. God was present and doing things in people's lives the like of which I've never seen before, and I've seen some things in my time, that's for sure. I know what went down, what I saw, what happened to me, what I did, but putting it into words is so hard. Probably the best thing to do is just tell it as it happened.

Just last night we were still making sure the doors were locked in case anyone should accidentally discover us. We'd been keeping a very low profile since Jesus was executed by the authorities. We were fearful for our own lives and just wanted to keep out of sight. We felt like frauds. He had told us that we were to 'go and make disciples of all nations', that we would be his witnesses 'in Jerusalem, and in all Judea and Samaria, and to the ends of the earth.' Yet, there we were, cowering away, fearful of being spotted and identified as having been with him.

Still, he had told us to wait in the city until the power came. But you can only stay cooped up for so long. It was the festival that did it. Someone said, and I can't remember who it was, that with Jerusalem so crammed full of pilgrims that no one would be looking for us. It was Pentecost, the Festival of Weeks. They said we could just blend in with the crowds going up to worship at the Temple and no one would be any the wiser. So that's what we did.

You have no idea what a different place the city is during a pilgrimage festival. Passover, Tabernacles they're all the same. It doesn't matter which one it is, people come from everywhere. There are thousands and thousands and thousands of people. It's like the whole of the world is here. Wall to wall people, some sacrificing, some just milling around, some praying, some teaching or listening to a preacher, others trading or just socialising. Actually it's all rather exotic with so many different languages and accents, far more cosmopolitan and open compared to the intense religiosity and strict orthodoxy of those who live here all year round. The fact that it's a public holiday has its own effect too, if you know what I mean. Anyhow, we waited for there to be plenty of people out and about before we ventured out onto the streets to go up to 'the House', the House of the Lord that is.

Progress was slow because there were so many people and the streets so narrow. However, when we finally arrived and had purified ourselves like everyone else in the Mikva, the ritual baths at the foot of the steps that lead up to Temple Mount, we made our way into the Outer Court. The Temple is such an impressive place. From the cramped confines of the city itself the Temple courts open out into large open spaces, large enough for the tens of thousands of visitors who come during festival time. The courts are arranged in terrace form, one being higher than another, with the Temple highest of all, so it can be easily seen from any part of the city and, as a result, it presents an imposing appearance.

The whole group of us were together as we began our festival worship there at the Temple. It was then that it began to happen. One moment we were giving thanks to God for the harvest and the next, well, we were caught up into the presence of God in a way that I have never experienced before. There were times when we were with Jesus that you just knew that God was so close. But this was different to that. They say that God's Spirit is like the wind, well, it was just as if he blew round us, through us and into us. The Psalmist says that God is a consuming fire, and it was as if that fire rested on us, but, like Moses' burning bush, we weren't consumed. It was incredible, heaven opened right there where we were sitting in the Temple and reached out and touched us, and filled us with his presence. In that instant, we knew that we were changed people.

This didn't go unnoticed. Goodness knows what we must have looked like but a crowd quickly gathered around us, keen to see what was happening. Some of us began to talk to them and try to tell them not to worry as we were only saying our prayers, but that's not what happened. We opened our mouths to speak and it was the strangest experience. It was almost an out-of-the-body type of thing. I wondered whether I had lost my mind. I heard myself making sounds that were just that, unconnected sounds. It was like being instantly struck dumb. No wonder some of them concluded that we were drunk, having started the day's celebrations early!

However, it soon became clear to me that these sounds weren't just the gobbledegook that I had initially thought. There was a pattern and structure to them, and a pace and rhythm too like real talking. Not only that, the foreigners who were listening nodded as if they understood everything that was being said to them.

It was only afterwards when we talked to those who had been there that we realised what kind of a miracle it was. I spoke to a man from Libya. He said it was amazing. His Aramaic and Hebrew are only basic so he struggles to understand what's going on when he visits Jerusalem. Suddenly, he said we began speaking in his own dialect and it was just like being at home. He understood every word as we spoke about the wonders of God's love and grace and mercy. And it wasn't just him. There were people there from all over the Empire. Goodness knows how many languages we spoke. Someone came up with fifteen different regions, but that was cheating a little because it included Judea too! One of our group said that he thought it was like the Tower of Babel had been reversed in that one moment. Like God was saying, 'I confused your languages thousands of years ago because you failed to obey me, but now I've got a message so important, I'll countermand that to get this message out.'

Anyhow, it was at this point that everything got really interesting. Some in the crowd were asking us what we were saying, what we meant, what was it all about – when some comedian made this quip about us having indulged in too much new wine. At the same moment, the twelve of us who had been closest to Jesus stood up spontaneously and Peter raised his voice to speak. But he was different. He had been a broken man after having denied that he even knew Jesus on the night he was arrested. He had been so disillusioned with himself that he was in danger of wallowing in self-pity. But now the self-loathing had gone. In fact, I'd never seen my brother like this. This wasn't the old Peter either; the impetuous hothead who would open his mouth before thinking and then regret having put his foot in it. No, he spoke with an authority and clarity that was commanding. Everyone's eyes were fixed on him and the people around us grew silent. He said that if they thought that it was just the alcohol talking they were wrong, and he began to explain what was happening by quoting the prophet Joel to them: '"In the last days," God says, "I will pour out my Spirit on all people. Your sons and daughters will prophesy, your young men will see visions, your old men will dream dreams. Even on my servants, both men and women, I will pour out my Spirit in those days, and they will prophesy."'

It was as if a window was opened into the heart and mind of God. It didn't matter which country you were from, everyone had been drawn to listen. It didn't matter if you were young or old, rich or poor, or even if you were a woman, this was for everyone. God was for everyone. No one was outside of his interest or care. His love is inclusive and all embracing. How could we have got that so wrong, so often?

As Peter spoke the number of people around us continued to grow. It must have been thousands by the end. The whole Outer Court was still and you could hear his voice echoing off the high walls that enclosed the area.

When he began to talk about Jesus you could see people beginning to make sense of it all. The last time most of this crowd of people had been together had been the Passover itself. They had seen Jesus for themselves. They had heard him teach and seen the miracles and the wonders and the signs with their own eyes. They had witnessed the crucifixion too; the authorities had made sure of that.

Peter was brilliant! He moved effortlessly from talking about what was happening now, to what had happened with Jesus and how it all related to the Holy Scriptures. But the climax was the resurrection. I can even feel the goose bumps on the back of my neck as I'm talking about it now. 'Wicked men put him to death by nailing him to the cross,' he said, oblivious to the fact that some of them who did it were standing on the edge of the crowd listening intently. 'But God raised him from the dead, freeing him from the agony of death, because it was impossible for death to keep its hold on him.'

Passionate and intense, with an eloquence that belied his lack of education and his thick northern accent, he spoke with a strong and powerful conviction, 'Be assured of this: God has made this Jesus, whom you crucified, both Lord and Christ.' And there it was; he acclaimed Jesus as the Messiah. The whole of God's purpose in history focused in this one person.

What happened then was incredible. Peter sat down and there was a stunned silence to begin with. It seemed like an age, but I guess it was only really a few seconds, and then it began. Some were groaning, others weeping openly. It was like someone had taken a knife and inflicted unseen wounds on the unsuspecting listeners. People were crowding round us all clamouring to ask questions and talk to us. One man was pulling violently on Peter's tunic shouting, 'Brothers, what shall we do? What shall we do? You've got to tell us, what shall we do?'

Peter got to his feet again and gestured with his hands for everyone to listen. 'Turn your lives around and go in a different direction,' he said, 'and begin by being baptised in the name of Jesus the Messiah for the forgiveness of your sins. Then you too will receive the promised gift of the Holy Spirit.'

Well, what followed was as exciting as it was bizarre. The obvious place to get baptised was in the Mikva at the foot of the steps that led to up to 'the House'. But you're only supposed to use them as you enter the Temple, not as you leave. So, people began to queue to use them on the way out. The attendants had never seen such a thing! And it wasn't just a few either. Hundreds began to wait in line. One attendant told me that it was almost comical to see. Those coming up to worship had no idea what was happening and just stood there bemused. Others tried to explain what was going on and had little impromptu meetings that recounted the events of the day. But there was no scuffling or bad temper. People waited patiently for their turn to step into these ritual baths, sprinkle a little 'living' water from the nearby Kidron stream and immerse themselves before stepping out, drying off, replacing their clothes and descending back into the city.

It took an age, but the attendant told me that he had estimated how many had used the Mikva in this way, and this is what I have found most difficult to get my head round, he said it must have been 3000 or more!

Jesus told us to wait in Jerusalem until 'the power came', but I don't know that we understood what he meant. But come it did, today, this power of the presence of God the Holy Spirit. And what an effect it's had. It certainly turned us around. From being nervous and anxious about the authorities identifying us as followers of Jesus, we publicly 'came out' in the Temple in front of thousands of worshippers. The Spirit enabled us to speak languages we had never learned to people we had never met with consequences we never expected with all these people getting baptised. Jesus said we'd be witnesses for him and that it would begin in Jerusalem. Today that's what we did. We told people what we had witnessed of Jesus' life, death and resurrection.

This day of Pentecost has turned Peter around too, and in the process turned him into a bold and effective preacher. It's strange how things come back to you isn't it? I remember Jesus telling us not to worry what we'd have to say when we were called on to talk about him and his message, but rather that the Holy Spirit would give us the words. Well, he certainly gave them to Peter.

But what I can't get over is the response. Nothing like this ever happened before, not even when we travelled with Jesus. What are we going to do with them all? There's so much they need to know, there are so many things that we'll need to tell them. Yet in just a few days they're going to be scattered back all over the Empire. But then I suppose Jesus did tell us just before he left that we were to 'go and make disciples of all nations'. Well, it's begun. Lord knows what lies ahead of us, but if the last twenty-four hours is anything to go by, it'll turn the world upside-down and inside-out. Can you believe it?

David and Abigail: 1 Samuel 25[1]

David: First narrative

I can't believe it! I just can't believe it! Of all the problems I have, I did not expect this one. Perhaps that is why I am so angry. With all I have to face, this is just one more thing. I don't need this now. It is not right! It is not fair! It is inconvenient, immoral, and unfair! In fact, it's just plain wrong!

After all, life has not been easy these past several years. Do you know what it is like to have your very survival threatened? It affects everything you do, the way you eat, the way you sleep (or don't sleep), and the way you think, and even your relationship with God. I am constantly looking over my shoulder, wondering what will happen tomorrow, almost afraid to go around the next rock. I struggle with depression and paranoia, wondering who are my real friends and who can I trust. It is times like this that reveal who are and who aren't your real friends.

Adding to all this stress and pressure is the responsibility of leading this large clan of people. I never thought I would

---

[1] This sermon has been developed by Paul Borden and his wife Teresa Flint-Borden. Paul is an educator and is presently Executive Minister for the American Baptist Churches of the West in California, USA.

be responsible for the care and feeding of six hundred men and their families. It is true most of the men are good men. I am convinced that a number would give their life for me. But in any group this size there are enough trouble makers whose antics just consume your time and drain your emotions. Not only do I have to worry about where our next meals will come from, keeping us safe and secure, but I am constantly arbitrating fights and arguments over the smallest stuff. And when you get right down to it, it is just plain greed! I sometimes have nightmares seeing all the women and children dead and no one is left alive. The pressure of caring for this mass of humanity, along with the stress of survival never, never, goes away.

Added to all I have just told you, is the constant warfare with marauding bands that have plagued my people for years. They have lived off Jewish sheep and grain while killing, maiming, robbing and raping. Shepherds, farmers, innocent people have lost their lives, their daughters have been taken into slavery, and poor people have lost the ability to make a living. In some ways it is exhilarating killing those who have made life so miserable for so many people. But, every time we go into battle, I wonder, who will we lose? Will we lose? Will I lose my friends? Who will die? Will I die? And then when it is over there is always the question of the spoils. First, will there be enough to feed us? Second, who will become upset because they felt they did not get their fair share?

Oh what I would give for those days when all I had to worry about was a few sheep. I know that I forget that those days weren't as easy as I picture them now. But I also know that the unrelenting pressure and stress I now feel was not there then. And back then I was not a wanted man.

That's what makes this problem so frustrating! It really didn't even have to be a problem. And what makes it even worse is that it is just so unfair. I mean, I know we do not live in a perfect world. Obviously life is not always pleasant.

But you at least expect people, especially those you have served so well, to treat you with some basic common decency. Well, let me tell you justice will be served!

After all, we did not have this problem with the other farmers and shepherds we had helped. We did our job and they recognised it, were grateful, and gave us our due. But no, not him! I guess I should have known better. He did have a reputation for being shrewd. I think that is why I had admired him so much. It is not easy to be a successful farmer on this land. You have poor soil, arid conditions, and not much grass for your flocks and herds. And somehow in the middle of all these conditions he had done more than just make a living, he was successful and rich. I was impressed. That is why, like other farmers and ranchers we had provided protection for his shepherds, his crops, and his herds. We had heard that his harvest festival was the largest in the entire area. I am sure he did this to display his wealth and success. That is why I had picked ten of my best men to bring back the gift. Actually it was our pay. I assumed his response would be generous since we had risked so much to make him even more successful.

You can imagine my response when my men not only returned rather suddenly, but empty-handed. I could tell they were embarrassed and scared to tell me what had happened. However, I urged them to tell me everything and they did.

They described the scene at the festival. It was everything we had heard about and even more. Animal skins were piled everywhere. Crops were heaped in piles. The threshing was going on constantly. There was the smell of roasting grain mixed with the odour of cooking meat. The place was busy, dusty, and exciting. Sitting above all of it on a platform, like some important king, was Nabal. He was giving orders, haggling with other shepherds, and obviously enjoying himself. It was clear that he was drinking but my men had watched him long enough to know that he was too shrewd to be drunk this early in the day. They assured me they had approached him with all due respect. They informed him about who they were, who they represented, and made their request. They reminded him of all we had done all year, putting our lives on the line for him and his people. You can imagine the shock they experienced when they heard his response. In fact I had to demand they tell me specifically what he said because they did not want to hurt my feelings.

He had waved his fat hand at all the harvest surrounding him and said, 'this is mine all mine, I have worked hard to produce all this and no runaway slave is going to come in here and take any of it. Who is this son of Jesse? Who is this David your master? You tell him to go back to his father and work for a living. He will get nothing that belongs to me! Now get out of here you begging sluggards and leave me alone!'

My men were so stunned they just left.

But I wasn't stunned, I was angry! After all, we had risked our lives time after time for Nabal and his people. We could have died. I knew what it was like to be alone with sheep when people wanted what was not theirs and I had no protection. We had given his shepherds what I had never had. And now to hear this, it is wrong, unfair and immoral!

I told my lieutenants, 'Get four hundred men and leave two hundred here to protect the women and children. We are going after Nabal. I will show him justice. I will teach that fat, arrogant, son of Belial a lesson he will never forget. By this time tomorrow he and all the males associated with him will be dead, or my name is not David!

Abigail: First narrative

I am sorry I do not have long to talk. My servant is bringing my animal and as soon as he does I must leave.

I have always dreaded harvest time. Oh, I know for most people it is a major highlight of the year. The festival is a time for dancing, good food, drinking, meeting and renewing friendships. I realise most people look forward the whole year to the festival. They can't wait for the smell of roasting grain and meat, pastries, fruit, and the sweets. For most it's a time for laughter, relaxing after a hard year of work, and enjoying life. In fact, I used to feel that way as a little girl. But for years now all the laughter, joy, and excitement of the festival have magnified the emptiness of my existence. I hate this time of year!

When I was younger, I was delighted when my parents had arranged my marriage to Nabal. It would mean a large dowry since he was already quite the successful farmer. And for me it would mean wealth, servants, a grand home, new clothes and the prestige of being Nabal's wife. I guess when you are young you idealise everything. Your dreams are coloured by fantasy and you never conceive that life is unfair. I assumed that Nabal would protect me. I knew that someone like him worked hard, was disciplined, and would be as committed to me as he was to his farm. He would provide for me and his new family in a style befitting his position. I was so happy the day of my marriage to Nabal.

But that happiness did not last long. My dreams and idealism were quickly shattered by reality. I soon came to realise that, to Nabal, I was just another acquisition like land or his animals. I was something to be bargained for and then consumed. Oh, he was strong. But he didn't use it for me. Instead, he just focused on more power and wealth. His pride was reflected in how he used me as his ornament to parade in front of other men. And he used his passion to control me and the children that came into our life. We existed to please him. I was to do just that in the kitchen and in the bedroom. When I didn't, I paid a price. I felt his power and strength too often in ways that now make me ashamed.

That's why harvest time is no longer a time of celebration for me. I have nothing to celebrate. Life is nothing but bitterness and frustration. My children bring me happiness, but now my sons are growing up to be just like their father. It is at harvest time that my husband's worst excesses are exposed. He brags about his success. He flaunts his wealth by throwing the largest and grandest celebration in the area. He bargains with weaker farmers taking advantage of their poverty and need. His pride is larger than the mounds of skins and grains he puts on display. His passion is evident as he feeds his ever increasing belly, drinks his wine, and sleeps with all the young women. I know how he brags to the men about his sexual exploits and they all laugh and go along with it because they fear his power and might.

However, this harvest he went too far. He crossed a line he should have avoided. Even I have now defied his authority. But when something threatens my children no one, not even that fat arrogant man I call my husband, will stop me.

Just a short time ago I was in the kitchen preparing more breads and sweets for the festival, staying away from the crowds as I always do, when Hezron our chief shepherd came in. He was trembling and his face was as white as bleached grain. I respected this man of integrity who took all the abuse my husband showered on all our servants and never said a word. He just did his job well day after day. He told me how David's men had come asking for the gift. Hezron told me that it was a proper request. He said that David's men all year had been a wall of protection for him and his shepherds. No one had lost his life and no sheep or cattle had been lost. He also told me that David's men had extorted no money or goods from anyone. He looked me in the eye and said, 'These are good men, they did us a great service and deserved to be paid.'

Hezron then told me how Nabal had humiliated and embarrassed David's men and sent them away empty-handed. Hezron started to shake. He said, 'I am convinced David is coming back to kill Nabal and when the killing starts I am afraid it won't end until we are all dead. I don't want to die and I surely do not want to see you or your children killed.'

Then Hezron shocked me when for the first time he spoke badly about Nabal. He said, 'He is a son of Belial and no one can talk to him or cause him to act justly.'

I grabbed Hezron by his shoulders and said, 'Look at me! Act quickly! You see all the food here, get some servants and put all of it on as many animals as needed and get them to take it to David. Do it immediately! Do not tell anyone what you are doing and if any asks tell them you are on an errand for me. When you are finished loading everything get my animal and bring it to me so I can follow you out to David. Now go. Go, I said, I must get ready!'

I can't believe I am doing this. I have never done anything like this in my life. I don't even know if David will accept my gift or not or even kill us. But I must try!'

'Hello, my darling baby. Mummy has to go out for a while. Find your nanny. Everything will be okay, I promise.'

David: Second narrative

I am quite familiar with injustice. I know what it means to have my motives misunderstood. I am all too aware of having my best intentions seen as being evil. As most of you know, King Saul thinks I want to kill him. Yet all I have ever done for him is kill his enemies, lead his army, play music for him when he's sick, and marry and care for his daughter Michal. Doesn't he realise that if I wanted him dead, he'd be dead.

Just awhile back, the king was on one of his usual treks looking for me and my men. We were hiding in this mammoth cave. It was not very smart really, when you think about it. I mean if Saul had found us, all his army had to do was block the entrance and we were dead. Anyway, we were hiding behind some boulders at the front when his army appears in the valley below us. They stop. At first we were scared. Then we realised they were just taking a break from their search. Meanwhile Saul starts up the hill to the cave. We realise he needs privacy. My men could hardly keep from laughing out loud. Here we are hiding in the back of the cave while our king is most vulnerable in the front of the cave doing his business. One of my men says, 'God has done this so you can finally get rid of Saul once and for all. Go and kill him now!' As I crept to the front of the cave I could just make out Saul's face. He seemed so old. He looked so tired and haggard. But as I looked at his face I knew I could not kill him. After all Samuel, under God's hand, had anointed him our king. He was the Lord's anointed for me.

But Nabal that filthy, stinking, fat, arrogant son of Belial is another matter. He is definitely not God's anointed. He's not even fit to carry his father's name. He is evil personified. It will be a pleasure to kill him and when I do, it will be sweet revenge for what he has done to me and my good men. I bet there will be much rejoicing when they hear of what I am going to do to that fat son of Belial.

'Come men, today we seek justice for us, for others, and for God!'

Abigail: Second narrative

I had just descended into the valley floor, more like a ravine really, when I looked up and saw the front of David's column of men. As they came closer fear gripped me. David, at least I assumed it was him since he was mounted, led them ever closer.

I knew all I had going for me was my words. So as we met I quickly dismounted and got to my knees and started talking. 'Oh, Lord, blame me, and what ever you intend to do to Nabal do it to me.' After all, I thought, I don't have that much to lose. As that thought hit me years of pent up anger just spilled out like a dam bursting and all I could do was speak.

'Forget Nabal. Don't pay attention to that worthless son of Belial. He is not worth your effort and he is just like his name, a fool. His life, his work, all he does repudiates his God and his treatment of people reflects nothing but selfish ambition. He is a foolish man. If I had known your men were coming I would have prepared the food you needed and even more. I am, no actually all of us, are indebted to you. You have served us well.'

I stopped speaking. David just sat there looking at me staring in amazement. Maybe he was shocked that a woman would talk like this or perhaps he just didn't know how to respond. But since he was quiet I decided it was best to keep on talking.

'David, surely you know that you are in God's hands. Samuel has told us that one day you will be Israel's next king. Nothing or no one is going to harm you. God has protected you as you led our armies against the Philistines. We all know that Saul hunts you constantly and yet never finds you. God is protecting you. Therefore don't stumble over a fool like Nabal. He is not worth your time and energy. When you become king you do not want his blood on your hands. Yes, he has treated you shamefully and I am sure you are deeply hurt. But still you have no right to kill him. When you are finally king and you have defeated your enemies, you want to rule with a clear conscience. Killing Nabal won't let that happen. If you have trusted God to help you with the Philistines and with Saul, trust him to deal with Nabal. If you take revenge you are denying God's ability to take care of you.'

David: Third narrative

I can't believe I missed it. Why is it that some things in life you see so clearly while in other areas you are so blind? I knew Saul's treatment of me was unfair and wrong. I have never done anything for him except support him and fight for him. Yet I knew in the cave I could not kill him. If I had, God would have dealt with me. Saul was my superior and God would have to deal with him. I saw that clearly.

But Nabal was another matter, or so I thought. He was this insignificant son of Belial. He was nothing to me. And he had offended everyone he touched. He needed to be disposed of; it would have been a service. But, I never realised that he was as much a part of God's plan for my life as King Saul. My faith in God had to be large enough to deal with both Saul and Nabal.

I must tell you that right now I feel so good. Nabal is dead and I am so happy. Wait, I did not do it. I don't know what happened but I have received word that he is dead. Yet I feel so clean since I had nothing, not one single thing, to do with his dying. Abigail was right, I needed to let my faith rule my emotions. Revenge would have felt so good at the time, but later it would have lain on my heart like bitter herbs on the tongue. And I almost missed it, and would have if it hadn't of been for her.

Abigail, what a woman! She has so much courage. I can't believe what she did sending the gift and then coming and confronting me. There is a woman who does not put herself first. She is beautiful. Oh I don't mean her looks. Ah, don't get me wrong she is gorgeous. But she is beautiful on the inside too. Nabal was a fool since he never realised what he had in Abigail.

Oh, I have sent for her. She and I are going to marry. Wow! Can you **imagine** having someone like Abigail for a wife? She is a woman of beauty and courage. She showed me how my faith is to be lived out even in the worst of situations.

Abigail: Third narrative

What a man! All my life I have wanted to be with a man who was strong. Not just physically strong mind you, but strong enough to face the truth even when it was inconvenient. I wanted a man who was proud, not of what he had accomplished but of how he could serve his God. I wanted someone who would be passionate for me and so passionate for his God that he would treat me well. Well, I now have such a man, David, and he wants to marry me!

Let me tell you I never thought this day would happen. You think I was scared when I met David, I was terrified when I went back to face my husband. I had experienced his abuse before, but now I had undercut his authority and he would be known as a man whose wife had made a fool out of him.

It was almost dark when I arrived home. I knew Nabal would be at the threshing floor. It made no sense to tell him then. He would be drunk and probably in the arms of a young girl. So I waited until morning. I got up early since I couldn't stand not dealing with it any longer. As I got to the threshing floor the signs of last night's debauchery were everywhere. Nabal was snoring, his big belly rising and falling with each breath. Food was caked in his beard and his breath was horrible. What a foul sight he made laying there. As I looked at him all I could feel was pity. What a fool.

As I leaned over to awaken him, his eyes parted slightly as the early light bothered him. I started by telling that David and his men had been on their way to kill him and us all. As I got to the part about what I did his eyes opened wide and his hands reached for my throat. All I could see in his eyes was hatred and anger. All of sudden his eyes rolled back into his head and he stiffened on the ground and just lay there as though dead. I gathered up a bunch of servants and with great difficulty we carried him up to the house. He never regained consciousness and after ten days he died.

And now David wants me for his wife. I will gladly be his wife and I will gladly serve him not only as his wife but as our next king. Here is a man who was willing to understand that God's work in his life includes the Nabals of this world. Who can resist marrying such a man of faith?

9

When the Preacher Uses a Narrative Form with a Non-narrative Subject

How Much Before Breakfast?: 1 Thessalonians 5:17

I have to begin today with an apology. Unfortunately, I'm going to make you all feel guilty, I'm really sorry about that, but there's no way of avoiding it. It's just that this is what's going to happen, it's inevitable. Unless, that is, you are one of those few people who have got it together. If you're not one of those few people who have got it together, then you have no alternative but to feel guilty!

Certainly, in my life as a pastor, I can say that what I am going to talk about is one of the most widespread and deeply felt problems among Christian people. It is indisputable that the vast majority of believers feel guilty about it and if they don't feel guilty about it, they feel they ought to feel guilty about it, and if you still don't feel guilty, I suggest you should examine your life with regard to the sin of spiritual pride and feel guilty about that instead!

You see, quite plainly and simply, what I want to talk about is our prayer life. In the Sermon on the Mount Jesus did say, 'When you pray, go into your room, close the door, and pray to your Father who is unseen, and your Father who sees what is done in secret, will reward you' (Mt. 6:6).

Jesus said it, but how often do we do it? This is the origin of the guilt that we feel. When I became a Christian in the mid-1970s it was drummed into us consistently that every Christian should have their daily 'QT'. If you were around then do you remember that, the 'Quiet Time'? And there are those really helpful groups like the Bible Society and Scripture Union who provide us with booklets of notes with an insightful thought for every day. The trouble is when you get behind and you have to do a catch up and do three or four days together. It can take hours! However, my spiritual mentor told me that it was good to persevere. I remember one time being told, 'Roger, it's good to form a habit of prayer, a godly habit. Why don't you try having your quiet time first thing in the morning, last thing at night?'

Well, I was game to give it a go, but I had a problem! First thing in the morning, I'm not alive! Mornings are not a good time for me. After my third mug of coffee I might just be about getting there, but by the time you've had time to drink that much, the day is well started, and people are ringing and knocking at the door, and there are meetings to go to. Then there is late at night. OK, it's quiet, there's nothing worth watching on the TV, so I settle down to pray and, do you know what? I go to sleep! My intentions are good and I'm down there praying, but the eyelids have gone, and that's it, I'm whacked out.

Whichever end of the day we seek to establish the daily habit, our failure to perform leads us to feel really guilty about it. And when we do manage to establish contact with heaven, and we trip off prayers like the one I was taught when I was little – 'God bless Mummy and Daddy, and Richard and Roger (Richard was my brother's name) and Grandma, and auntie so and so, and my rabbit, Nibbler …' – we have a strong sense of the inadequacy of the prayers we pray, even when we do manage to pray them.

We are just about dealing with that, when some really smart preacher speaks on prayer. In the process, they quote someone they know or some great prayer warrior of the past, who rises at six and prays for two hours before breakfast. Whether that is John Wesley or George Muller or some other great saint, the problem is, rather than encouraging us to get up at six to have two hours before bacon and eggs, we just feel even guiltier because we don't perform it at all and apparently there is no hope.

So, having dealt with the smart preachers and their guilt-inducing sermons, we start reading the Bible. But that's always a fatal mistake! You get into the Gospels and you discover that from time to time Jesus didn't even go to bed! He stayed up all night and prayed the whole time. We try to imagine what it would be like if we did that. What we would be like at work the next morning or coping with the children as we try to get them ready to go off to school. As a consequence, we get totally paralysed with our own inadequacy in prayer and our inability to do anything about it.

Now, let's be real. It's not as though we don't want to pray. We're Christians after all! Jesus has become our special friend, we've invited him to have a central place in our lives, but there is an obvious implication. We really can't be much of a friend if we allow him to get so squeezed out. What kind of friends are we? And at the base of it all, most of us, most of the time, run with a really low self-image of how we are with the Lord. If we are honest with ourselves, we conclude that we can't be much of a disciple with a prayer life as non-existent as ours.

Then just when we're feeling particularly inadequate, along comes someone who is really all fired up. They've been to a conference; or, they've heard a life-changing sermon; or, they've read something in the Bible; or, God has taken them in hand and their prayer life has taken off. They seem to be managing thirty hours of intercessory prayer each day, and spending the rest of the time in Bible study! Their excitement and enthusiasm, rather than inspiring us to follow in their example, sends us completely down the 'plughole'. And then to cap it all, we hit a verse in 1 Thessalonians 5:17, where Paul says, 'pray continually'. Now you could read that as regularly; but if you were to read it as regularly, you would be misreading it. Paul wrote a very specific Greek word for continually. The word is *adialeiptoos*, which means 'without interruption, without ceasing, incessantly'. Without interruption, without ceasing, incessantly? What does he want? Are we supposed to be monks and nuns? Maybe 24/7 is the only way to pray without ceasing, but it means going without sleep too!

If that is the mark we've got to aim for, it is unobtainable. None of us can handle it. Maybe that's God's plan. He wants us all to feel perpetually guilty about it, because we don't pray continually, without ceasing. Real prayer is therefore always beyond us. Maybe that is what God wants. Unless, that is, Paul is talking about some thing else completely.

What is prayer, actually? Talking to God? OK, but that knocks silent prayer on the head, doesn't it?

I remember one time I was wrestling with this whole issue. We were living in Manchester at the time. I was training to be a minister. Just over the road from us, we had a large park – Platt Fields, if you know Manchester. Well, one day, I was walking in the park, wrestling with this. I remember saying to the Lord, 'Lord you know that my prayer life isn't up to much.'

At the time I was spending half an hour to an hour praying each morning before I went into College for breakfast. And I said, 'Lord, I am just so dissatisfied – it really isn't together. What can I do?'

It was as though he said to me, 'Roger, what is prayer?'

Now I often have conversations with God like this, in my head. You might begin to think that I've lost it here, but I do! And he said, 'What is prayer, Roger?'

'Well, it's having my quiet time.'

'No, more basic than that,' he says.

'OK! Talking to you?'

'No. More basic than that, Roger.'

'How do you get more basic than that?'

'Well,' he says, 'what do you do when you pray?'

'I talk to you.'

'Before that.'

'Before talking to you? Well, I come into your presence.'

'Ah, you come into my presence. Now you see it. Prayer is being in my presence. That's how you can pray without ceasing, Roger.'

You know how it is sometimes, a little light suddenly goes on inside your head and you understand. It was crystal clear. Praying without ceasing, praying continually for me meant living my whole life in God's presence, as if he were by my side. Of course, it's not 'as if' at all. He has promised to be with us always hasn't he?

Then a whole pile of Scriptures began to fall into place for me, or at least, for some, the lack of a whole pile of Scriptures fell into place. Do you know that you can search the whole of the Gospels, in fact the whole of the New Testament, and in no place will either Jesus or Paul or John or Peter or anyone else tell you that you have to have a daily quiet time with God? I guess that God must have really slipped up there if he wants us to religiously have a daily set time with him.

Now, don't mishear me! There is in the Scriptures, teaching from Jesus about getting alone with God. We've already looked at it, Matthew 6:6, 'When you pray, shut the door, pray to your Father in secret.' But there is nothing about a strike rate there at all; or how regularly we have to do it.

Then there is that brilliant passage in Romans 8:26–27, verses that confound a lot of people. They wonder what they really mean. Paul says, 'In the same way, the Spirit helps us in our weakness. We don't know what to pray for.' Does that sound about where you are at? Paul goes on, 'But the Spirit himself intercedes for us, with groans that words cannot express and he who searches our hearts, knows the mind of the Spirit, because the Spirit intercedes for the saints in accordance with God's will.' Now there are at least ten sermons in those two verses, but Paul is saying that prayer goes beyond words. It's not just talking. It's also taken up with those inward groans that you can't even **begin to express. Another translation talks about sighs too** deep for words. The Holy Spirit prays within us.

Now, as Christian believers, when we come to faith, when we invite Jesus to be a part of our lives, the Holy Spirit comes to live within us. Paul says here that the Holy Spirit helps us in our weakness. We don't know how to pray but he prays for us. He uses those groans and sighs that are beyond words, on our behalf, to form intercessions because we are so weak at prayer!

This week I have been with a number of people who have really been in life's hard places, having lost someone they love. Now I know it hurts and I know it leaves emptiness, but how do you effectively and really pray? Pious platitudes are hollow and serve no one. But in our weakness, the Spirit prays with groans too deep for words. I have been with a number of other people who life has assaulted violently and consistently. I have never been in that place. I have no idea what it's really like. My heart has gone out to them; and the Spirit, seeing my weakness, intercedes with groans too deep for words.

Only one thing will stop us living in God's presence in this way, when we block his presence out of our lives by the wrong choices that we make. When we entertain something that is out of order, when we sin, when we turn our back on God, when we don't do what he has told us to do, and we do what he has told us not to do. When we lie and steal and cheat and gossip and lust and are greedy for things. The list goes on and on. You've heard enough about these things over the years, you ought to be at least beginning to be aware of what they are. These things block off our life with the Lord so that the Spirit can't intercede. Our responsibility is to keep our life clear, so that the Spirit can use us in the circumstances in which we live. As long as we walk with God, our whole life becomes a prayer at a spiritual and sub-conscious level.

Again, don't mishear me! I'm not saying that conscious prayer is unimportant. I'm not closing the door on closing the door and getting consciously alone with God. That kind of prayer is important. Neither am I saying the formation of godly habits is bad. On the contrary, they are good. But rather, what I am saying is that we have pumped these things too high. We have set a standard that few can attain and we have all felt guilty about it as a consequence. Rather than inspiring intercession it has impeded the real life of prayer that is inspired by the Spirit day by day and hour by hour.

We have failed to understand the life of prayer and what it's all about. We have gone with the outward sign and how long we've spent praying, rather than recognising the inner reality. We've judged ourselves according to the exception, the one who is called to stand in the gap, the one who has a ministry of intercession, rather than by what Scripture says, that which God would teach us. That prayer is not so much about talking with God as it is about intimacy with God.

When Paul wants to talk about the relationship between God and the church, between the Lord and the believer, he uses the illustration of marriage and the relationship of husband and wife. In doing so, he follows the Old Testament which speaks in the same way. The relationship of a husband and wife in its intimacy takes time. My wife and I have been married twenty-five years this year. Our relationship and our intimacy together as a married couple have taken time to grow over those years. Back in the mid–1990s we spent more time apart than we had ever done in the past as I regularly travelled from the UK to the United States and was away for weeks at a time. In a relatively short transatlantic phone call the intimacy of our relationship is automatically in place. We discovered that we didn't have to spend hours and hours on the phone to re-establish things because we hadn't spoken at length for a few days. Do you see it?

Our prayer life with God is not about the length of time we spend in prayer, but rather it is about the level of our intimacy in our relationship with Him. This is important.

There are times when I spend hours talking to some people and I've wondered if we have communicated at all, let alone at any depth. It's not about length of time; it is about the quality of communication and the depth of the relationship. That's what prayer is really all about.

Intimacy is about openness and depth, not hours and minutes. Paul tells the Thessalonians to, 'pray without ceasing'. That's about living our whole life in the intimate place in the presence of God. It's about allowing the Holy Spirit to pray through us in all the circumstances in which we find ourselves. It's about keeping our lives clear and clean before God.

Effective, conscious prayer on your own with God in the privacy of your own room with the door shut is exactly the same. It is based on the depth of our intimacy with God, not in the hours and minutes we log up rehearsing words. It's not about the hours we spend before breakfast. It is about the intimacy of our relationship with God. It's not about the length of time we spend praying, but it is about the quality of our communication.

One of the things we will discover as we begin to explore what God has to say about prayer is that we actually begin to be liberated to pray. No longer watching the clock to see how many prayer minutes we've clocked up judging ourselves according to the exception. No longer striving to measure ourselves against the one called to a ministry of intercession, the one called to 'stand in the gap' as Ezekiel 22:30. Not viewing ourselves in the light of the exception, but rather seeing our prayer as flowing out of the intimacy of our own relationship with God. These prayers flow out of the experience our lives with God and they have substance and depth because, beyond our words, the Spirit has the freedom to pray through us in our weakness.

There are times for personal prayers when we will close the door and pray to our Father in secret. Then there are occasions when we will spend time praying together openly, audibly, consciously. It's good to form both of these godly habits, but it is a backward step to become a slave to them.

What matters is that twenty-four hours in every day we are living in the presence of God; allowing the Spirit to intercede in our weakness. He has freedom to be at work in our lives because our hands are clean, our hearts are pure and our relationship with God is open; at home, at work, in school, in college, when we're shopping, doing aerobics, when we're living in our neighbourhood, whatever we're doing, wherever we find ourselves, every moment, every day, is lived in God's presence.

I said that you'd probably feel guilty today. As far as we perceive our own inadequacy in prayer, the temptation is to feel guilty. But prayer is not about how long we spend on our knees before breakfast. It's about how intimate we are with God and how much our life is open to him. Prayer is not about how long we spend in conversation with him, but is about the depth of our relationship with him. Prayer is not about a heavy burden of religious piety that we can never ever live up to, but rather is about a spontaneous, living, vital relationship, that we share with him in the totality of our lives.

Paul and Mars Hill: Acts 17:16–34

You are where you normally find yourself to be. That may be at work or at school or wherever you normally invest your leisure time. Some like golf, others badminton or shopping, whatever, you are in one of those places where you normally find yourself. Then, someone you're with turns around and says to you, 'and so there's just no point to my life!' You realise in that instant that you have the opportunity to speak about Jesus and share the good news of the gospel. Who knows, you might even lead them to the Lord. At that precise moment in time your heart skips a beat, you feel faint, your mouth is taken out of gear and your brain freezes over. By the time you've regained some semblance of internal order the moment is gone and the conversation has moved on to what was happening in yesterday's soap opera. Why do we do that?

Or there comes one of those announcements from the front of the church that volunteers are needed for evangelism. Now it's one thing to be part of a group of 50 or 60 going down to the shopping centre to sing, but it's quite another to be sent out in twos to accost people on the streets and to witness to them personally. It's one thing to do a house to house distribution of leaflets or even to go with a survey form to find out what the people in the local neighbourhood think. People like to have their views marked off on our sheets. However, it's quite another to commit to participating in door to door evangelism, to speak of the four spiritual laws and to ask that leading question, 'Well if you died tonight do you know where you are going to end up?'

So why are we like that? Why do we back away from evangelism? What is so intimidating about sharing our faith when there is an opportunity that presents itself?

Now I've heard some good reasons over the years. I can think of three categories that these excuses normally fall into.

The first one is: 'It's not something I feel called to; it's really not my gift.' This one actually sounds like my family after dinner when the dishes need doing. 'It's not my turn.' Basically we're saying, 'I don't want to do that thank you very much.' It implies that it's somebody else's responsibility. We have found within our family that the dishes are everybody's responsibility and therefore we have a rota to make sure that everyone pulls their weight. The responsibility for evangelism, to be witnesses, is one that falls on us all. 'It's not my gift' is just an over-spiritualised way of saying, 'I don't want to be involved in that, thank you very much!' Jesus said to all of his disciples, 'You will be my witnesses.' He didn't make it a special commission for a select few; neither did he make any exceptions. This was something they were all to be involved in.

The second excuse I've heard is: 'I'm not very good with words.' Ha! You should hear them with their friends. They chat away like old pros. Not very good with words my foot! You could even put them down in the middle of a foreign country and, even if they did not speak the language, with a few gestures they could make themselves understood.

I have also heard people say, 'I don't understand the faith well enough.' Well that might be excusable for the new Christian, although often they seem to be the very best at talking about their faith. However, the people I hear saying 'but I don't really understand my faith well enough' have often been Christians for years. Are they ignorant or something? What have they been doing with all those sermons they've been listening to? What about all the Bible studies they've taken part in, the books they've read and the personal devotional time with the Scriptures they've had? How come they still don't understand the faith?

Maybe it's a comment on those of us who are preachers and our quality of preaching.

Actually, we don't have to be a walking encyclopaedia of Christianity to share our faith. When I spend time with groups of new believers I spend time letting them know that it's OK to answer 'I don't know.' The longer I live as a Christian the more I realise that there are many things that I don't know.

Here's the nub of the problem. Sharing our faith with someone is not about having all the answers so much as it is about sharing our experience of God. It's far more about talking through how Jesus has been 'good news' for me than it is about knowing the correct theological answer to the mystery of theodicy (by the way, that's what the theologians call the problem of suffering).

Even a new Christian can talk about their personal experience and the impact that Jesus has had upon them.

Our problem is altogether deeper than our attempts to sidestep the issue with our excuses. Let's face it, as good as we make our excuses, when it comes down to it, we feel guilty when we don't get involved in witnessing, evangelism and sharing our faith. And if you don't feel guilty – well you ought to because the rest of us do.

So, why do we feel so guilty? Well, I guess one reason is because preachers have been telling us for years that we should be sharing our faith.

Then there are those who write books and tell stories about the great triumphs of personal evangelism. There is the story of the evangelising jogger who gets up early to jog round the neighbourhood, claim each street for Christ by prayer as he jogs and has three people converted before croissants and orange juice. Or, there is the executive who, on his train journey into the centre of the city, converts at least one person per week from the conversations he has with the people who sit next to him. Then there are those wonderful parents who even at the school gate seem to be able to bring the parents of the other dear little kids to faith.

And as if that is not enough, then there are the Scriptures. Jesus sends out seventy of his followers in twos to proclaim the good news. In Acts 1:8 Jesus commands all the disciples to be his witnesses first in Jerusalem, then in Judea, Samaria, and to the ends of the earth. It's no wonder we feel guilty when we don't do it.

Then there's that instinctive thing. We just know it's what we should be doing anyway, whatever anybody else says. You only have to hear the stories of people who have recently come to faith to know the longing that it awakens within us. **We want to share our faith with others** too. We want to see more people making a commitment to Christ and coming to experience the faith that we have found in Jesus.

So, why is it when we are told we ought to do it; when we know we ought to do it; when we feel like we want to do it; we are equally sure that we don't want to do it?

Those who have no fear about sharing their faith seem to be from a completely different planet to the rest of us. They appear to be insensitive to all the things we feel that make us so anticipant and anxious about it all.

If you have ever felt this apprehension about sharing your faith, as I have, think about it for a moment. What's it all about? Do you know what I've found (and I have always had a heart for evangelism since I was called to work in the church as an evangelist back in the late 1970s)? I have found that at the bottom of my hesitation to share my faith, I am frightened. My problem is quite simply, common or garden fear.

I am frightened that I wouldn't know what to say and how to answer the questions that would be put to me.

I am frightened that I wouldn't know my Bible well enough.

I am frightened that I'd be in the middle of a conversation and my mouth would hang open and I would appear completely ignorant.

I am frightened because it is an uncomfortable and embarrassing experience. Just look at the people who seem to do it all the time. Their confrontational and 'in your face' style as they begin to share and talk about Jesus is just not me. I'm not made that way. It might be OK for famous preachers to hit potential converts over the head with a Bible, but I have to continue to live here and see these people tomorrow and next week.

I am frightened because I might be misunderstood. I might be seen as someone a little bit nutty when I'm desperately trying to be a normal person.

I am frightened that I might be labelled as someone who has 'got religion'. And that can be devastating. Maybe you have heard recently of the story of what happened when a number of footballers in an English league soccer team became Christians. They were immediately transferred because faith was not conducive to that particular dressing room.

I am frightened at making myself open and vulnerable and risking rejection. You know how it is at the dinner table at work. You sit down and begin to unpack your sandwiches to eat and your colleagues, having seen it was you, move to another table. Or you try to talk to them and they just turn away and don't even answer.

I am frightened of being mocked, being called names, and being victimised by the pranks that are so often focused on those who don't fit in.

Now, this is what I'm thinking. If my problem is fear and I was called and set apart to do the work of an evangelist, I guess that's what a whole a lot of people are feeling and experiencing too.

Of course, the apostle Paul never had this problem – Paul the great apostle of the faith and courageous advocate for the gospel. His story makes every believer quake in their shoes at the thought of even following in his footsteps.

For the sake of the gospel of Jesus, Paul says,

> I have worked much harder, been in prison more frequently, been flogged more severely, and been exposed to death again and again. Five times I received from the Jews the forty lashes minus one. Three times I was beaten with rods, once I was stoned, three times I was shipwrecked, I spent a night and a day in the open sea, I have been constantly on the move. I have been in danger from rivers, in danger from bandits, in danger from my own countrymen, in danger from Gentiles; in danger in the city, in danger in the country, in danger at sea; and in danger from false brothers. I have laboured and toiled and have often gone without sleep; I have known hunger and thirst and have often gone without food; I have been cold and naked.
>
> (2 Cor. 11:23–27).

And so he goes on. I guess we could be forgiven for thinking that Paul didn't know the fear that we experience, having been through so much.

Let me share a thought with you, actually I suspect Paul felt exactly what we feel. He tells the Corinthians that, when he arrived in their city, 'I came to you in weakness and fear and with much trembling' (1 Cor. 2:3). Hallelujah! Paul's experience corresponds with ours.

So, if I feel it, and you feel it, and even the mighty apostle Paul feels it, this fear, where do we go from here? How did he, that great evangelist, that tremendous missionary pioneer extraordinaire, front it out? Actually, it was really very simple, so simple that we can miss it. We can pass it by and get the wrong ideas into our heads. Luke records Paul's speech in Athens at the Areopagus and there is an important clue there. Listen to what he said:

> Men of Athens! I see that in every way you are very religious. For as I walked around and looked carefully at your objects of worship, I even found an altar with this inscription: TO AN UNKNOWN GOD. Now what you worship as something unknown I am going to proclaim to you. The God who made the world and everything in it is the Lord of heaven and earth and does not live in temples built by hands. And he is not served by human hands, as if he needed anything, because he himself gives all men life and breath and everything else. From one man he made every nation of men, that they should inhabit the whole earth; and he determined the times set for them and the exact places where they should live. God did this so that men would seek him and perhaps reach out for him and find him, though he is not far from each one of us. 'For in him we live and move and have our being.' As some of your own poets have said, 'We are his offspring.'
> Therefore since we are God's offspring, we should not think that the divine being is like gold or silver or stone – an image made by man's design and skill. In the past God overlooked such ignorance, but now he commands all people everywhere to repent. For he has set a day when he will judge the world with justice by the man he has appointed. He has given proof of this to all men by raising him from the dead.
>
> (Acts 17:22–31)

Simple, isn't it? Well, not so clear to us maybe, but if we had been members of the Areopagus it would be plainly obvious. Quite simply, Paul met his listeners where they were. It is as simple as that.

Let me explain. The Areopagus was a group of thirty men. It was the most exclusive council in the greatest university city in the world. They would sit in judgement on cases of murder and personal morality but their greatest delight was in being a debating and philosophical talk shop.

In Acts 17:21 Luke records that all of Athens was given to talking about the latest ideas. Then along comes Paul, but because we are not first-century Athenians we don't hear what he said. If we were, we would hear him at one point angling what he says towards Stoic philosophy. At another, we see how he speaks the Old Testament truths in language that those who had studied Plato were familiar. At one turn he is quoting Epimenides, while at another he is using Aratus and Cleanthes. If we were sitting in this grand court Paul would be speaking to us in our language.

Paul could do that because he was an educated Roman citizen. He met the people of the Areopagus, those thirty men, exactly where they were. He was able to do that because he understood them. He had studied these scholars and poets too. There was a connection between him and his audience.

This pattern of meeting people where they were is one that has been developing throughout the Acts of the Apostles up to this point. He arrives at a new place. He immediately goes to the synagogue and he meets those believers in Yahweh. Starting with the Old Testament he speaks to them about Jesus. Then he arrives in Athens. He begins with the synagogue as usual, but he also goes out into the market place. The market place was something like a Speakers' Corner in London. People would stand up on their 'soap boxes' and would talk and debate and get into disputes and they loved it.

Paul met them where they were and they were so impressed he gets invited to the biggest and most prestigious council in town to speak of his new ideas. And here he speaks with Platonic and Stoic philosophy in mind, referencing his ideas to Aratus, Epimenides and Cleanthes. He meets them where they are.

Here's an important point, we don't have to be frightened that we won't know what to say. The people that we share our faith with are part of our time and culture, as the men of Athens were a part of Paul's time and culture. What we need to learn to do, if we need to learn at all, is to speak normally and naturally as we do in everyday life, living where we live. As someone once said, 'If Jesus came to London he'd probably have a Cockney accent!'

A while ago I was flying over to the United States, to Denver via Houston. I was sitting next to a businessman who was going over on a business trip. This trip was 9½ hours and, of course, you are sitting next to the same person for the whole trip. Well, we sat down and were beginning to talk and exchange pleasantries when he asked the question that no pastor wants to be asked. "So, what is it you do?' I was going to have to sit next to this man for hours and was a little reticent about how the news of my occupation would be received. However, I was always taught that honesty is the best policy so I just let it out, 'Well, actually I'm the minister of a church.' 'Oh, that's interesting,' he said, and we just talked for virtually the full time. No great shakes. Sometimes we were talking religion, sometimes we were talking about his job in computers, sometimes we were hardly talking about anything meaningfully at all, but it was normal and natural. Over the flight I must have had half a dozen or more opportunities naturally and spontaneously to talk about the deep things of life and the difference that Jesus has made in my experience. There was no need to be fearful or uncomfortable about it, it was an easy and flowing conversation. There was no need to be fiery eyed, intense and confrontational either. Actually, it was all rather friendly!

This is how Paul begins too. He doesn't stand up and point at the council and rail at them, 'You sinners, turn to the living God and repent of your wickedness!' No, when he addresses the Areopagus he says, 'I see that in every way you are very religious.' He begins by complimenting them. And just to show how much he'd begun to take in, he says, 'I see that you have a statue TO AN UNKNOWN GOD. Well, what you worship without knowing, I'm going to tell you about.' There is no confrontation or conflict at all. He meets them where they are.

We don't have to batter people into submission and jump down their throats to share the good news of Jesus. Now let's have a clear impression of this story. Not every one who heard Paul speak was converted. In fact, in Athens Luke tells us there were only a few who made a positive response. Others seemed open to continue the dialogue further at a later date, 'We would like to hear you again speaking about this' they had said to him. However, there was a negative reaction too. Some of them sneered. I guess they were mirroring those in the market place who were calling him a 'babbler'.

We can never escape the possibility of rejection or worse as it will always remain a reality for those who choose to follow Jesus. Indeed, Jesus himself sought to prepare his disciples for the inevitable. 'Remember the words I spoke to you: "No servant is greater than his master." If they persecuted me, they will persecute you also. If they obeyed my teaching, they will obey yours also' (Jn. 15:20).

While we cannot sidestep rejection and possible persecution for our faith, God still uses our attempts to meet people where they are as we share the good news of the gospel. In Athens it may only have been a few who came to faith, but come to faith they did. Dionysius of the Areopagus was one of the elite, one of the top thirty men. We do not know much about Damaris but, as women had a very restricted role in

Athens at the time of Paul, she can only have heard him in the market place. If that was so she may well have been a woman with a dubious reputation.

Meeting people where they are is not only a gospel principle given to us by Paul. Indeed, it is the very example that God gives us in the incarnation. We don't have to claw our way up to heaven to reach to God, because in Jesus God came to meet us where we are. And that's the secret to evangelism.

The problem with meeting people where they are is that contemporary culture is continually moving on. That means our evangelistic strategies need to continually move on too. At the end of the Victorian era magic lantern shows and brass band music were very successful as means that enabled the gospel to be presented. The latter was incredibly important in the growth of the Salvation Army. However, they wouldn't 'cut it' today because that's not where people are at in our contemporary culture.

Door to door evangelism began as a response to the early city life following industrialisation when traditional communities were broken down and the urban poor were living in horrendous slum conditions. And that was just 150 years ago, particularly in London but mirrored throughout the UK and USA. Those who still practise door to door evangelism find it to be one of the least profitable evangelistic activities. Faith Popcorn, the American cultural commentator, talks about how people are now 'cocooning' their home environment and do not want it invaded by uninvited outsiders. Indeed, I know how I feel when a salesman comes to my door and interrupts my home life with things that have no interest for me.

The question that we must wrestle with, as every other generation has done, is how do we meet our contemporaries where they are today? A former colleague of mine who headed up the outreach of a church that I used to pastor used to constantly tell us that knowing Christ was the answer was the easy part. What we had to discover were the questions of our generation? Such a discovery then takes us a long way towards understanding how to share the gospel most effectively in our context, with our friends, with our neighbours, with our family, with our work colleagues. And we do that by being normal people. We don't need a degree in evangelism. We need to be the people we are, to meet the people around us, where they are. We inhabit the same world, and our conversation will veer from politics, to TV, to sport, to sport on TV, to the fact that there is too much sport on TV, to the soap operas, to the experiences we have in every day life, the incidents we remember.

Just recently, my wife, Marion, and I were invited out to dinner and as Christians we were the minority around the dinner table. I wasn't looking forward to it. The conversation cut in and out of the World Cup, education, economics, and even religion. As we talked in that context we had a very real opportunity to share the good news of Jesus in a low-key way.

Wherever you find yourself in the coming week there will be some topic of conversation that has a direct or indirect religious dimension. Look out for them. Be ready to say, 'Well, as a Christian I think …'

These issues impact us as a church too. I guess the Lord alone knows where we shall end up, but it's interesting to see some of the things that various churches are getting involved with for the sake of the gospel.

Some are getting involved in caring for people struck with Aids and are earning the right to speak of the good news of Jesus among the homosexual community. Many have experimented with very different forms of service that are 'seeker sensitive' and far less 'churchy' so that Joe Public, when he walks in through the door, will not feel totally disorientated by what we do. There are some believers who are opening stalls at New Age fairs because there are a lot of spiritually open people attending such events. I even know of one church that releases its minister and a number of members to go to car boot sales on a Sunday morning to meet people where they are.

That's what it's all about, meeting people where they are. And where they are, is where we are. Where they live is where we live. We inhabit the same space. Rather following the latest religious marketing strategy than with formula answers that are learned by rote as some do, we need an altogether different approach. Sharing the good news of Jesus is actually about being the people we are, living where we live, doing what we do, meeting the people around us, where they are, living where they live, and doing what they do, as the people they are. It's as simple as that.

We will always have to deal with the fear of rejection for that's living with reality. But, as for the fear of what to say and how to say it, that's not such a big deal. If it is about meeting people where they are, as Paul did at Athens, then we are on home ground. For Paul at the Areopagus it meant having knowledge of Epimenides, Aratus and Cleanthes. For us, well as we meet people in the local shopping centre, at the school gate, or at work our talking will more likely be filled with what happened on Oprah, the latest goings on in the Big Brother house, or what we saw on last night's news. And when we chat about these things with those we know and talk about the reality of the faith that we have found in Jesus, we'll be doing exactly the same as Paul. We'll be sharing our faith as we meet people where they are.

Part 4

Preachers' Insights

10

Voices from the Pulpit

'The proof of the pudding is always in the eating!' At least that's what my old grandma used to say, and she certainly knew about puddings. The principle holds true in the ministry of preaching too. No matter how logical the theory of narrative preaching sounds, how biblical the practice appears or how compelling the conclusions are, if it doesn't stand up to scrutiny in the pulpit it is worse than useless.

How does it feel to preach in a narrative style? Is it so different to prepare for? How do congregations respond? What impact does it have upon the preacher? These are just some of the questions I put to a group of individuals who have already tried their hand at preaching in a narrative style. Having been invited to share candidly from their experience they give the insider's eye view. The group is made up of ordained and lay preachers, from Britain and America and of a wide spectrum of experience. Some, like Paul Borden who introduced me to narrative preaching in the mid-nineties, have been using the style for years. Others, like Richard Hibbert, would confess to only ever having preached a handful of narrative sermons and therefore being at the beginning of acquiring a new skill set as preachers of the gospel. I am grateful to them for willingly opening up their successes and their failures and being prepared to

put them down on paper for others to learn from. What follows are stories and reflections from their own experience.[1]

1. What first got you interested in narrative preaching?

Richard Hibbert
I was asked to speak at an Ash Wednesday service, but one
of the staff said, 'Could you be more interesting than just
giving us a three point sermon? What about leading a meditation?' I found myself praying about the subject matter,
and turning away from the traditional Ash Wednesday
texts. I settled on Zacchaeus in the end, as it was about
repentance and inner transformation. Then I pondered
what angle I would take on the story and decided to narrate
it as if I were Zacchaeus. I remained faithful to the general
thrust of the storyline but found myself trying to get inside
the character, inside his feelings, his expectations, his

---

[1] Dr Paul Borden is the Executive Minister of the American Bap-
tist Churches of the West, San Ramon, California, USA.
Pastor Bryan Clarke is the Senior Pastor of Lincoln Berean
Church, Lincoln, Nebraska, USA.
Rev Aled Edwards is Churches' National Assembly Liaison Offi-
cer (CYTUN, Churches Together in Wales), Cardiff, UK.
Rev Ian Hamlin is the Minister of Hayesford Park Baptist
Church, Bromley, Kent, UK.
Rev Richard Hibbert is the Vicar of the Anglican parish of Christ
Church, Bedford, UK.
Rosemary King is a teacher and serves as a Reader in the Anglican
parishes of Ryton-on-Dunsmore, Bubbenhall and Baginton,
Warwickshire, UK.
Major Mike Parker is Secretary for Personnel, Territorial HQ,
Salvation Army, London, UK.
Sue Taylor is a lawyer and serves as a reader in the Anglican
parish of St Stephen's, Buckhurst Hill, Essex, UK.

frustrations, his joys. I asked people to close their eyes, relax and let the story carry them. As I finished, I was conscious of incompleteness. About a minute of silence followed and then, without warning, one gracious and godly listener suddenly started speaking quite profoundly about the story and its call upon our life. It was clearly divinely inspired as neither he nor I had liaised beforehand, though people presumed we had, and his five minute word from God beautifully completed what I had felt was so unfinished. It was a divine moment.

Rosemary King

For years I have been using Ignation-type meditation on a Bible passage for my private devotions and on retreat. One of the Ignatian techniques for getting into a passage is to use your imagination to see the scene in detail, perhaps through the eyes of one of the participants. Then you might hold an imaginary colloquy with that person, letting God speak to you through what the biblical person says in your imagination alongside the questions you ask and your response to what is said. This works so well for me, that one time when I had a sermon to prepare, I thought I would see if this kind of approach would bring the passage alive for my congregation, and help them to hear what God might be saying to them through it. So I prepared a narrative sermon in the first person, and it worked!

Ian Hamlin

When it comes to sermons I'm not a great listener. Though not from a Christian family I was sent to church from an early age and my abiding memory is of being bored. Even today, I often find myself distracted when listening to someone else preaching. On my good days I get caught by an alternative point in the text, but more frequently by some odd feature of the church or the congregation. As a preacher

I remain slightly embarrassed about this and am desperate not to be dull. Of course, these considerations are secondary to my passion for the contemporary relevance of the biblical text and the need to communicate effectively within the postmodern milieu (chuckles)!

Bryan Clarke

I first became interested in narrative preaching when I began to analyze the communicators that seemed to be effective versus those who were not. I wondered why it was that some could hold my attention so well and others caused my mind to wander. It was clearly not an issue of personality or volume. I noticed it was not always even a matter of content either. There were times when speakers would speak on a subject I had little interest in but I would find myself engaged to hear what he or she had to say. Over time I came to realise it was the narrative form the material was packaged in that was appealing to my sense of wonder and discovery. Narrative communication takes the listener on a journey with the speaker to resolve the tension intentionally established at the beginning of the presentation. Rather than wondering 'why are you telling me this', I found myself engaged with a clear idea of where the journey was headed.

Mike Parker

Having served as a church leader for five years, I was appointed to the Training College of The Salvation Army as a Sectional Officer. One of the responsibilities was to teach homiletics. The material I collated and the research I conducted not only challenged but inspired me to look at more creative ways of preaching the Word. Having a personal history in reciting and monologues, it was not a difficult transition to develop an interest in narrative preaching. From those days of training others, I continued to proclaim the Word of God in many and varied ways, narrative preaching being one of them.

Aled Edwards

My local incumbent and mentor encouraged me to preach from a very early age. As a teenager, with a great deal of support and supervision, I could do nothing other than tell my own faith story and pass comment on the faith narrative of other Christians. In my case, there was another reason why I embraced a narrative-based approach to preaching. At school, I encountered what modern educators would now identify as a specific learning difficulty. Seeing the written word before me in a pulpit proved to be more of a hindrance than help. I found it much easier to preach without notes when I was story telling than with a more abstract subject. So, as a consequence of this disability my preaching has been heavily dependent on story telling from the beginning.

Sue Taylor

I didn't realise it was narrative preaching. The label came later. I was trying to tell a particular Bible story in a way in which listeners could become part of the story and understand what was going on, perhaps identifying with a character or finding a new perspective on the story. It isn't my normal style so that probably startled a few people too!

2. How different do you find preparing a narrative sermon to a more traditional one, and why?

Mike Parker

For me, the preparation of narrative preaching material takes on a different format to the more traditional exposition of the Word. In the latter, I tend to approach a passage or theme by gently tapping at the material until the 'diamond' hopefully appears. Questions are asked, 'What is the text saying?' 'How does it relate to today?' 'What does God want to say to his people?' 'How does it resonate with where they are in the life that they live?' By contrast, in narrative preaching I tend to try and get into the story. Rather than seeking to explain the passage I try to get into the characters and let the story explain itself.

Richard Hibbert

I find myself reading and re-reading the text more, not in order to pull it apart and to discover its constituent parts, its flow of argument and its textual interests, but rather to feel my way into the story. I particularly want to begin to recite the story as if I were the original narrator, picking up the feel and nuances in the text. I also want to read and re-read the story so that I became very familiar with it, so that as I write my narrative sermon I don't need to refer to it. I notice that in my preparation the insights from the commentaries are counterbalanced in a new way by a fundamental need to reflect more on the emphasis of the story.

Rosemary King

It's much more creative and intuitive, and fun. A parishioner said to me one time when I preached a narrative sermon from the perspective of Samuel: 'I enjoyed your sermon, Rosemary, and I could see that you were enjoying it too.' That's not to say that I don't enjoy preparing and delivering more conventional homilies as well: I do. And although preparing a narrative sermon is more like, say, writing a short story, it isn't the same, because this is the Word of God you're presenting to these people. And so you have an absolute responsibility to be faithful to the text.

Homilies tend to be more based on my logical thought but narrative sermons let me trust the Holy Spirit to lead me, as he uses my imagination to put the ideas into my mind that he wants these people (and me too) to hear. Trusting the Holy Spirit is risky, but infinitely rewarding and exhilarating.

Writing a narrative-style sermon often involves me with lots of research: probably more than a homily: the historical and geographical details have to be right, for example, and the details I need can send me cross-referencing all over the Bible and church and secular history too. This is in itself a stimulating process, which brings the biblical text alive for me, so that hopefully, God can use me to bring it alive for his people.

I had a very interesting experience one time when I had a sermon on John 20:19–29 all typed up and ready to go. When I woke up the day before I was due to preach it was as if this imaginary Thomas inside me was trying to get my attention and begging to be let out to talk to the people himself. So I got up and sat at the computer and let my imaginary Thomas talk. The original sermon is still in my 'Sermons not preached' folder; I may use it sometime; it wasn't a bad sermon.

Ian Hamlin

I find preparing narrative sermons takes far longer and is much harder – though often more enjoyable. Digging into the roots of a story, in particular its characters can be an almost unending process across a range of disciplines, with all the time-consuming consequences. My training still forbids me from inserting any creative detail I can't reference, or saying anything at all that I would struggle to justify and this adds to the workload. For this reason alone I would struggle to prepare narrative sermons on a weekly or even fortnightly basis.

Bryan Clarke

The key to narrative communication is establishing the tension up front then taking people on the journey to discover the solution for themselves. Both narrative and traditional preaching styles include a proposition. The difference is that narrative seeks to create tension up front and present the proposition at the end while the traditional approach states the proposition up front and explains, defends or applies it. In many ways, the traditional approach lets the air out of the balloon up front and leaves little mystery to the rest of the presentation. One of the most difficult things to do in preparing narrative-styled communication is determining the plot of the presentation. What is the tension point to be delivered up front? In other words, why does it matter what I'm about to say? Sometimes getting into the skin of the listener and processing why they need to know about what I'm about to tell them is the hardest part of the process.

Mike Parker

I have learned to preach from my own life experience. Self-knowledge is the root of all great storytelling. A storyteller creates all characters from the self by asking the question, 'If I were this character, in these circumstances, what would I do?' The more we understand our own humanity, the more we can appreciate the humanity of others in all their good versus evil struggles. Great storytellers and I suspect great preachers are sceptics who understand their own masks as well as the masks of life. They see the humanity of others and deal with them in a compassionate yet realistic way. That duality makes for great preaching.

One of the most powerful illustrations of this for me was when I took a group of young married couples on an evangelistic campaign in the east of Scotland. Each was given the task of entering into a character from the Gospels and, in essence, giving their story from the point of view of that character. Each of the characters would tell their story to the point of challenge that came through Christ. Each ended their story with these three words: 'Then Jesus came.' At the end of the fifth and final character presentation the three words were uttered, 'Then Jesus came' ... and he did! There was a movement of the Spirit amongst the congregation as many came forward to confess his lordship in their lives.

3. Do you find any significant differences in your presentational style in preaching a narrative sermon? What are they?

Mike Parker
Preaching in a narrative style has in many ways enabled me to become much freer and independent of my notes as I feel less comfortable handling papers when engaged in narrative preaching. It therefore demands greater preparation and a greater dependency on God. In a way, it has both given to me and brought out in me a freedom in preaching which has also touched other styles I use.

Rosemary King
Yes, I have noticed that speaking though the persona of another character in a first person narrative gives me the confidence to be much more direct – even confrontational – in speaking to the congregation, than I would normally dare to be speaking as their lay reader!

Aled Edwards
Good narrative preaching is far more than a process of telling stories and providing pictures. The Welsh language has

a word for that terrible condition when a preacher gets too fond of his own voice in a pulpit. Wales has perhaps enjoyed far too much hwyl. For me, the genius of narrative preaching rests in the seeing and listening – not just in the oratory of the telling. In primary school I was taught by an exceptionally talented young teacher. As a child with learning and communication difficulties I always admired his ability to draw cartoon pictures and write poetry. In a poem he wrote entitled Yr Afon (The River), he craves for the child's ability to 'see a voice and hear a picture'. Good narrative preaching rests on that gift, in the context of an encounter with God, to 'see a voice and hear a picture'. The communication flows from this.

Richard Hibbert
The differences are that a narrative sermon on the surface seems less about rhetoric and oratory and more about storytelling techniques. In a sense the dramatic pause and the speeding and slowing of speech are just as integral to storytelling as to a traditional sermon. However, the importance of painting a picture, of unveiling the story piece by piece and seeking to draw the listener onto the edge of their seats is much different to a more traditional sermon where one might lay out the road map in advance.

Ian Hamlin
Yes, naturally the narrative style gives the opportunity to take on different voices – to be someone other than a preacher with my particular style. But on the whole I've found the narrators voice to fit quite well with my own natural conversational style. I imagine that this has been a part of the attraction for me.

4. How have your listeners responded to this different style? Do you understand why?

Paul Borden

Some years ago, while teaching preaching with Haddon Robinson at Denver Seminary, he asked me to take a week of meetings for him due to a sudden illness in his family. In light of the fact that I would be preaching both mornings and evenings at a Bible Conference for a week, he and I agreed that I should preach a series of sermons based on narrative passages. I was teaching in this area and had developed several such series.

The Bible Conference was attended primarily by older people who had the time and resources to be there. The very first sermon I did was a third-person narrative based on several passages in Mark's Gospel. When I finished no one came to me to offer any reflection on the sermon. In fact the entire crowd purposefully avoided talking to me in any way. I went back to my room and shortly thereafter there was a knock at my door.

The man standing there said he wanted to speak to me. He informed me that those at the conference were used to expository sermons and that what I had done did not in any way fit their understanding of exposition, even though I had exposed the text far more than I could have in any other way. He then informed me that there was no way I could compete with the great speakers that had been at the conference the last few weeks. However, I definitely needed to change my way of preaching. You can imagine my chagrin and sense of failure. The rest of that day was not my best one by a long shot.

That evening I preached a 'regular' type sermon from 1 Samuel. After the sermon people came up and expressed their appreciation for my message. The man who had talked to me caught my eye as I was leaving and gave me a 'thumbs up' gesture indicating that I had preached appropriately. I smiled but inside I wanted to say and do things to him that are not appropriate for Christians to say or do.

This experience taught me that for many Christians the form of the sermon has become as absolute as the biblical text being preached. The result is that people often lose out on rich new ways of doing good Biblical exposition because they have become trapped in assuming such preaching can only be done one way.

Rosemary King

I've only had positive comments. Added to which, you can tell by the way they look as you're preaching that they're alert and engaged, not finding the next hymn, yawning or dozing. I have found that congregations tend to be looking up and making eye contact. This is probably because, when you hear narrative there's always the 'I wonder what comes next?' factor to keep your attention engaged. Also, of course, if the preacher is engaged, interested and enjoying the whole experience that's infectious as well.

Having thought about why this should be I have concluded that narrative preaching provides a way to relate to people from the pulpit in a non-didactic, non-threatening, non-patronising way. For those who do know the background well, hearing it again in narrative form has got to be less tedious than hearing a quasi-lecture about stories they learnt at Sunday school.

Ian Hamlin

'That was different.' 'That was unusual.' 'That was interesting.' 'I'd never thought of it like that before.' 'You made me think today.'

There always seem to be more comments than usual, most often positive, frequently intrigued, challenged, entering into the debate within the story. Rarely though do they compliment me formally for the sermon, almost always there is a seeking to continue the telling of the story. Perhaps that means the focus is in the right place.

Bryan Clarke

One of the great benefits of narrative communication is that it engages both hostile and apathetic audiences. On one occasion, I was invited to speak to a gathering of teenagers in a public school environment. Knowing this as primarily a secular environment with little spiritual interest I had to determine a way to motivate the teens to listen to what I had to say. The topic was dating and marriage. As I approached the audience their lack of enthusiasm for my presentation was obvious before I opened my mouth. Either they already resented what they thought I was going to say or they simply didn't care. To open with a clever story then state my case would have sealed my fate in the first minutes of my talk.

I decided to use a narrative form of approach. In the first couple of minutes I invited them to consider the home they were growing up in. Was it happy? Was it all they hoped it would be? Would they like to experience the same relationship with their spouses as they saw in their parents? Would they desire to treat their kids the way they've been treated? Having created the tension at the beginning of developing the plot, immediately there was a reaction. Audibly they answered my questions with obvious disgust and anger towards their home experience. I had hit a hot button. They made it clear both verbally and non-verbally they did not want to repeat their current experience.

That tension opened the door for me to suggest if they don't want to repeat what they are currently experiencing they need to consider some different choices. I was then able to discuss issues of morality and relationships, and they listened and considered what I had to say.

Was it effective? Many students wrote to me in the weeks that followed thanking me and telling me their story. One wrote: 'You taught me some very important messages about what should come out of marriage and the best way to make things work. Thank you for coming. I know you really made some people including me sit back up and realise where life is going.' Another wrote: 'I really think you had a lot of good things to say. It touched my heart when I knew for sure that there are people out there like you.'

Richard Hibbert
After one of my first narrative sermons, members of the congregation who spoke to me about it said that they had found themselves taken up by the power of the Old Testament story and had been fixated by the creative edge. I think those who are more creative enjoy the storytelling, finding that it speaks to them, whereas those with a more reasoned approach to life prefer sermons that give them logical expositions. Perhaps in the end it is all about learning styles and personal preferences.

After that early attempt at a narrative style sermon one of my churchwardens made what I felt was a positive comment: 'Very interesting presentation and thought provoking, but don't do it regularly!'

Aled Edwards
My overall impression is that narrative-based preaching falls far more gently on the modern ear than a more formal sermon focused on abstract theological concepts.

5. What has worked well for you, and why?

Sue Taylor
For me, it all has to do with being able to identify with a character, If I can't get inside them I cannot take others

there either. I find it easier, therefore, to go for personalities or feelings.

When I preached on the Parable of the Ten Minas in Luke 19, it became the story of the man with the empty handkerchief; the man with no confidence, who daren't take risks, who let the others rush off full of ideas and enthusiasm. The one who wrapped up the money given to him and hid it so he didn't have to think about it, at least not yet. Only to find that all he was left with was the empty handkerchief and the wish that he'd had the nerve to have a go. The surprising element for me was how I came to sense his regret at not having the nerve to have a go, how it really was hard for him even though it was so easy for the others. That this was a feeling many identified with was confirmed by the feedback afterwards.

Richard Hibbert

I have found it particularly refreshing to preach in a narrative style and not be forced to have to squeeze an Old Testament story to fit into the linear argument of an exposition. Those non-linear thinkers in the congregation have equally found the stories speaking afresh to them and linear thinkers have had to reflect more on what the text says to them personally rather than have the preacher's perceived application offered. Maybe it offers God some scope to work in people's hearts!

While being faithful to the text, I have enjoyed recasting the story, especially if it is well-known, reworking the plot to recreate the original vividness of a well-known passage. I believe that strategically using the narrative form has brought alive a sermon series by offering people a varied diet of teaching.

Bryan Clarke

One environment where I've tested the power of narrative often is at weddings. People come to experience the wedding not to listen to the preacher talk. This creates a very difficult environment to get a message heard. It's easy to get something said but often hard to get something heard. The solution for me has been to put myself in the shoes of those attending and consider what would immediately get their attention at a wedding without seeming out of place in such an environment. I've found many couples who attend weddings remember what they felt at the altar years ago but have not found their marriage to be as fulfilling as they thought it would be. I use that to raise the question of why and then map out the plot of my narrative sermon from there. I consistently get comments from people attending these weddings related to how that has caused them to think and reconsider the path of their lives. In less than ten minutes, the narrative form creates a tension and solution that connects with people.

Rosemary King
I can't think of a narrative sermon that I've done that has not worked well for me. They have mostly been first-person narratives, because I love the directness of the first-person perspective. Anglicans are normally required to preach 'to the lectionary', which means that the congregation will have already heard the Biblical passage on which we are required to preach earlier in the service, probably immediately before the sermon. Most biblical narratives are third person, so switching to first person for the sermon gives a different perspective and prevents people from thinking that I'm just retelling the Bible text.

Ian Hamlin
Generally, I've preferred working as a third-person narrator. I've felt it easier to include additional relevant information that way without appearing too contrived. Sometimes I've voiced a character from within the story but

using the past tense, to have him reminiscing, to achieve a similar effect. One time, I did Abraham reflecting on his journey up the mountain with Isaac by his side.

Once, we put on a short workshop at our church on storytelling and narrative preaching. An older lady came along who was a faithful believer – the only one in her family. She had always been quiet and was only rarely willing to put herself forward. She would attend every prayer meeting but would almost never open her mouth to pray.

Having attended the workshop, I invited her to share the story she had composed. It was an account of the last supper from the perspective of a waitress/servant girl and I planned to have it in the place of the communion prayer at our next communion service. To my surprise, she agreed and told the story – with immense truth and power. She was encouraged and the church challenged. The appeal of narrative is contagious.

Paul Borden
Some years ago, I did a biographical sermon about the Apostle Paul based upon the section in 2 Corinthians 11 – 12 where he describes all the suffering he had gone through and then talks about being caught up into the third heaven. I dressed in first-century garb and played the Apostle as an old man talking about how God has used suffering in his life to advance the gospel and to keep him from becoming proud. Since it was a first-person narrative, I did not talk about where all these events were found in Scripture. I also did not want to tick off a list of suffering, as the Apostle seems to do in chapter eleven, since I wanted the audience to feel what he must have felt experiencing all these events. So I just described what my life had been like in bringing the gospel to people and how God had led me whether the events were good or bad.

The week after preaching the sermon, I encountered a man in our church who had faithfully taught the Scriptures to others for years. He told me that once I was into my role he knew the passages I was using. He then related how he had opened the text to 2 Corinthians 11 – 12 and followed along. He was amazed that I had not missed one event in the Apostles life even though I had not always followed the order of events as Paul had written them. He said you must have memorised that entire text. My response was that I had not even tried. I told him that I had wanted to become Paul and that I had visualised all of these events from the Apostle's perspective and tried to imagine living them and responding emotionally and spiritually to all that had happened. The result was that I had not missed one event on the list despite the number of happenings Paul describes.

True first- and third-person narratives enable me to move from memorizing material to making it my own, living it and then relating the Biblical material to people through characters that become real. I do not memorise the events of my life since I have lived them. When I preach in a narrative style the same becomes true for the character I am playing.

6. What has not worked well for you, and why?

Mike Parker
I remember one of my first attempts at narrative preaching. I had taken the story of the shipwreck of Paul in Acts 27. Preparing on paper was fine, but I 'lost the plot' a little on delivery. Having told the story from Paul's viewpoint, I could not help myself at the end of the sermon and slid into an exposition of the passage. Having the joy and privilege of a spouse who shares the ministry is of invaluable benefit. After the service was over she said very clearly that the Lord had spoken powerfully through the narrative preaching. It

was a shame that I had to get in the way by explaining what God had already explained to the hearts of the congregation. I did not make the same mistake again!

Richard Hibbert

I have tried the narrative style for a theme rather than following a biblical story only once and felt I had not done it true justice. My theme was 'Standing up for the hope we have in Jesus', reflecting on the context of an adult baptism. My narrative was partly personal and partly followed the homiletical plot idea of Eugene Lowry. It wasn't particularly polished, but I realised that this style of preaching is quite different to how I normally preach and that it requires far more thought and practice than I had realised. Not starting with a passage of Scripture also does give a less certain feeling to what one is trying to get across when you are schooled in the more traditional form of expository preaching.

Ian Hamlin

I have found first-person-narrative sermons particularly hard. I don't think I have the acting talent for it. I find I can only sustain it for so long.

Rosemary King

I have heard the comment about a sermon, thankfully not one of mine, 'he just retold the Bible story. The trouble was, the Bible told the story better.' The Bible is indeed a hard act to follow.

Bryan Clarke

On one occasion, I told a story to create a tension at the beginning of the message and left it unfinished as I moved into the message. Those who were familiar with my preaching style knew it was alright because I'd finish it eventually.

However, in the conclusion I forgot to come back to it and finish the story. I left them hanging. Afterwards, I was bombarded with people wanting to know how the story turned out. I realised on the positive side that the narrative form is effective because it had kept these people tied to the message to get resolution to the story. However, if the tension is so great and not resolved it is possible they will forget everything else that was said. In this case, they were so wrapped up in the story they did not really hear the rest of the message. There is only one thing worse than having no tension, and that is creating tension and not delivering any resolution. There are times when people will say, 'You raised this question in the beginning, but you never really answered it. Now I'm more confused than ever.' These are some of the risks with narrative when we don't do it well.

Sue Taylor
I have found that narrative preaching doesn't work for those of a strictly logical way of thinking. Partly, I guess, it's easy to slip out of the biblical narrative to add a few details to fill out the story, which irritates some. 'How do you know the master looked at him sadly on his return?' Even when following the text strictly I was challenged that this method of preaching imposes modern thinking on ancient culture; how do we know how people of that time thought or reacted? To which I would say that it doesn't matter if by doing so we can find a lesson for today and if the speaker makes it clear at the outset that he or she is inviting the listeners to enter the story to find that lesson. It's also hard to add in historical data or Greek derivations for those that value those in a sermon. So it is not perhaps a style to use every week.

7. What things would you want to share with other preachers who are about to experiment with this new style?

Mike Parker

I have learned that in narrative preaching, God can speak very powerfully through the story itself and not through any of my perceived wisdom. Let the story speak!

It would be a fair analysis to perceive that many preachers struggle to communicate effectively. In an age of PowerPoint and visual aids, where people spend more and more time in front of the television and watching films, the traditional exposition of Scripture can, at times, seem banal, boring and dry. Sermons can often be greeted with cynicism, lassitude or outright dismissal. The challenge, perhaps, is to engage the congregation at a new level so that they can engage with God and God with them. Telling the story is a method which can do this at a very personal and emotional level. With this in mind there are three things I would highlight.

First, engage people's emotions, tell the story well and you will arouse people's emotions and energy. Harness their imagination and you will bring vivid insight into your story and exchange the yawns of your congregation to open-eyed appreciation.

Secondly, relate the story to the aims of your message. Good narrative preaching describes what it is like to deal with some of the big issues which our people face – for example, Jonah and the whale: rejection, remorse, repentance; Paul and Silas and the Philippian jailor: fear and freedom. You will be challenging your congregation to dig deeper and discover the truth for themselves. Stories have been implanted within each of us many times since our mothers took us on their knees. Cognitive psychologists describe how the human mind, in its attempt to understand

and remember, assembles the bits and pieces of experience into a story beginning with a personal desire, a life objective, and then portraying the struggle against the forces that block that desire. Stories are how we remember.

Bryan Clarke

People today seem to feel the need to use Microsoft PowerPoint and other visual devices to present their outline as they speak. This reflects an attempt to reach a visual audience with a literate presentation. What the audience craves is not a visual outline but a plot that takes them on a journey. The visual stimulation that people crave is not a static display of an outline but a story created in their imagination that takes them on a discovery journey. In my opinion, PowerPoint roots people in the here and now. This works against the aim of narrative preaching. I don't want people to be stuck in the here and now; I want them to come with me and get lost in the journey. Every time the computer clicks up a new screen the audience is aware we are in a formal presentation that is lasting x amount of time.

There is a need to remember too that a more traditional approach is sometimes best. For example, when the speaker is trying to prove something it may be better to state the proposition up front then seek to defend it. In such a case, clarity is more important than creativity. There may be times when the subject matter is of such interest that it creates its own tension and can be best communicated in a straightforward propositional form. However, many times the hardest task of the speaker is to convince the audience they need to listen to what the speaker has to say. This is the heartbeat of narrative communication.

Often when people think of narrative preaching they think of telling stories. Stories are a form of narrative but narrative is certainly much greater than mere stories. Narrative is a speaking form that organises material in such a way that a tension is created at the beginning of the presentation and resolved at the end. The meat of the message is dedicated to taking the listeners on the journey to resolve the tension. This creates the plot. Narrative is not so much the telling of a story so much as a plot that is developed and investigated from the beginning to the end of the presentation.

Richard Hibbert

First, while being creative never overdo it. It is very easy to 'over-egg' a narrative sermon.

Secondly, make sure that what you say remains faithful to the thrust of the passage you are retelling.

Thirdly, offer an inexperienced congregation some guidance of how they might handle the experience of a narrative sermon, or else they could end up 'all at sea'.

Ian Hamlin

Don't worry about not being able to come up with a narrative sermon every week.

Be prepared to give it a go even if you feel you could have done more preparation – there is always more that could be done.

Resist the voice in your ear of that college lecturer trying to tell you its not exegetically appropriate!

Rosemary King

Meditate on the passage, using Ignation or other meditative techniques, whatever you find helpful in personal prayer. Sleep on it, go over it in your mind as you drive to work or wait at the bus stop. Immerse yourself in it.

As with any sermon, ask the Holy Spirit to use you to speak to his people. He has called you, inadequate as you are, to do this work for him, so he's going to help you.

Relax with the subject matter. Let the creative juices flow. Go with the flow, go where he leads you.

Enjoy!

8. How has narrative preaching changed you?

Ian Hamlin
It has caused me to enjoy preaching more, to appreciate my Bible more and to be refreshed in its ability to stir and challenge a congregation of all ages.

Rosemary King
It has increased my confidence as a preacher: I can do this thing and it speaks to people. It has made me more trusting and open to God's leading – the process is creative in much the same way as painting or pottery or poetry is creative. And when we are creative we reflect, in our own small way, our Creator.

Richard Hibbert
It has freed me up from the need to always produce a three-point sermon. Old Testament passages seem better if allowed to speak for themselves, as they were originally intended.

Mike Parker
Narrative preaching has added another dimension to my ministry. It has challenged me to keep working at ways of communicating relevantly to an ever increasingly sceptical world. It has encouraged me to understand that 'God in His wisdom has made it impossible for people to know Him by means of their own wisdom. Instead, by means of the so-called foolish 'message we preach', God decided to save those who believe' (1 Cor. 1:21, GNB).

So I encourage you to 'Go and tell' the stories.

11

Been There, Done That!

It was over a decade ago that I first heard of narrative-style preaching. I remember sitting on the edge of my seat as I listened to Paul Borden speak of Jesus walking the shore of the Sea of Galilee and ministering. I was caught up in the story and entranced in a way that I never had been before. I was walking the shoreline too. It was an energising and exciting experience. Here were new and effective ways to communicate the gospel message that I had not begun to explore in my twenty years as a preacher that had led up to that point.

Ten years on what have I learnt? What does a preacher beginning to contemplate launching out into preaching in a narrative style need to have in mind? Four things strike me from my own experience and reflections on preaching in a narrative style.

Be Careful When Introducing a New Preaching Style to Your Congregation

I guess that I have been a little surprised at how some have responded to different styles of pulpit ministry. When I first began experimenting with narrative preaching I was the pastor of a church that had been marvellously open to change. We had sought to take the whole church with us in repositioning ourselves to being relevant and accessible to those who would not normally darken the doors of a church. The congregation had proven itself to be both willing and open to try new things and were, on the whole, patient with me as their pastor and tolerant of my attempts to explore new ways of doing things. This was why I had not expected some to struggle so much with narrative-style preaching.

I had been doing the same level of preparation as I did for a more traditional sermon and had sought to incorporate the exegetical insights I gained into my sermons. Still, Jane and Gladys were concerned enough to ask to speak with me. They shared how a number of people in the fellowship were troubled by these trendy sermons that might be 'tickling people's ears' but were rather short on Christian teaching. There was nothing malicious or undermining in what they did. They cared for their pastor and were very loving in the way they sought to communicate their concerns with me.

The church had a long tradition of expository preaching of the highest calibre when I took up the pastorate in 1990. I had failed to appreciate the need to introduce changes to the preaching style more carefully to enable some of the more established members to make the transition. Because we were open to change in almost every other area of church life I had presumed that it would not be an issue. I have learnt that we need to take special care in this area because the normal style of preaching is so central to the life of a worshipping congregation, especially an evangelical one with the emphasis on the preached word of God, that, while many in our congregations will welcome fresh styles of pulpit communication that are more attuned to our experience in contemporary culture, this response will not be universal.

The unity of the church always has to be a high priority for those of us who are called to leadership within the body of Christ. There can be no doubt that preaching, as much as any other dimension of church life, can benefit from the insights of the management of change. These insights enable people to walk the path of innovation together with understanding. For the want of a little forethought and preparation why would we do it any other way?

Narrative Preaching is Not the New Jerusalem of Homiletics!

There is a temptation to see every innovation as a 'cure all' for the many problems we face. Those of us who become enthralled by new ideas and insights can easily commit the cardinal sin of the convert to a new idea and get everything out of proportion. Certainly there are strong reasons to believe that preaching in a narrative style can significantly aid our preaching. The argument of this book has been that it is a more culturally sensitive style that is far more familiar to those who listen to our sermons than more traditional forms. It also has the advantage of being a biblical style too.

It is easy to be seduced by the dramatic response of some within our congregations the first few times that they hear a narrative sermon. Julianne had been in church most of her adult life and was an enthusiastic Christian. A thirty-something with a lively mind I was thrilled when she came to me after one of my first narrative style sermons and said, 'Roger, that was amazing, I have never felt so drawn into a story in the Bible and it spoke right into what's happening to me right now.' We talked together and prayed and she went home excited that God was at work in her life.

It is good and sobering to remember that in the early days of experimenting with a narrative style much of the response can be down to the novelty of a dramatically different pattern of preaching than anything else. When we have been preaching in this way for some time our congregations will be more familiar with it and its impact will not be as exaggerated.

There is a lot to be said for bringing variety to our practice of preaching. Certainly this is the experience of our congregations in the everyday world. Communication comes in a whole galaxy of different styles. We are very sophisticated consumers of messages from the wide world around us. The Bible uses a range of different literary styles across its sixty-six books. It may be that one significant way to keep our sermons fresh in the ears of our listeners week by week is to vary the style in which we preach. Whether it is topical preaching, verse by verse exposition, doctrinal sermons or one of the other homiletical styles, each has a part to play in providing a rich and healthy Sunday diet for the Christian community.

Falling in Love With Narrative

While I am convinced of both the biblical legitimacy of preaching in a narrative style and its cultural appropriateness, I have to confess I do not preach purely narrative style sermons as much as I initially thought I might. I suspect that part of this is due to the relative ease of preaching according to established habits. In addition, there can be no doubting the fact that narrative is far more demanding to write well.

In conducting follow-up research with participants at a one-day seminar I led for the London Institute of Contemporary Christianity I was fascinated to discover that others share my experiences. One year on, I made telephone contact with them to find out what their experience had been over the ensuing months. All but two of the participants reluctantly admitted that they had not even attempted a full-blown narrative sermon. For myself I have noticed a far greater ease in using the narrative form with non-narrative material in regular Sunday ministry than for opting to use a first- or third-person narrative. I suspect that this is because it is closer in style to the traditional forms of preaching and is therefore easier to deploy.

Almost without exception those I telephoned spontaneously also told another story. They had fallen in love with narrative. While they might not have experimented with the more formal narrative style they spoke of how their understanding and appreciation of narrative had taken off. They told of how it had impacted their telling of the Bible stories themselves within other sermon forms and, indeed, how other anecdotes were also coming alive in new ways.

When I was training to be a preacher, like many others I was encouraged to read novels. This I was told would help me understand the human condition. So, over the years I have never felt guilty about investing time in reading a good book. From James Herriot's tales of a veterinary practice in Yorkshire to the courtroom dramas of John Grisham and classic tales of Dostoyevsky I have devoured novels over the years. However, since my interest in narrative has been awakened it is not only the insights into people that have helped my preaching. I find I am captivated by the whole event of communication that storytelling encapsulates. I go to the cinema now far more than I used to, and I love to listen to a good storyteller on the radio. Garrison Keillor, Alistair Cooke or the excellent stories on BBC Radio Four's *From Our Own Correspondent* have become essential listening and a delight since I fell in love with narrative.

Yet narrative preaching is not merely good storytelling. In the UK gospel storytelling has had something of a renaissance, especially within the stream of spirituality that has drawn life from the Celtic tradition. Storytelling should have an honoured place among us for we constantly need to rehear 'the gospel story'. Narrative preaching has similarities with storytelling, yet it is profoundly different at its very heart. It is the preacher's proclamation of God's Word rather than just a storyteller recounting the stories of our tradition. It carries with it all the spiritual disciplines of preaching that for me are summed up in the introduction to this book, i.e. it is:

- A missiological imperative.
- Preaching the Word of God – a biblical word.
- Truth through personality – an incarnate word.
- Audience focused – a contextualised word.
- Collaboration with the Holy Spirit – an inspired word.

Can a Preacher Act in the Pulpit?

Back in the 1970s, the Anglican preacher David Watson enabled many British evangelicals to reintroduce drama into the proclamation of the gospel. He would pause in the middle of a presentation for a dramatic sketch to be performed that illustrated his theme. 'After these sketches I found it so much easier speaking,' he said, reflecting on the contribution that Paul Burbridge and Murray Watts brought to his mission work.[1] Out of this early work together The Riding Lights Theatre Company was born and acting began to flourish within worship services in the UK.

Having been enthusiastically involved in a church-based amateur dramatics group during the 1970s that was committed to producing reviews with both sacred and secular themes, I have always had a positive attitude towards the use of drama in worship. I had been glad that David Watson

---

[1] David Watson, *You are my God*, 136–8.

had helped to establish and broaden the manner in which drama could be used in a worship service. Having been on the organising committee of the Merseyside Christian Festival in Liverpool which he led in 1979 I can clearly remember now how 2000 people in the Empire Theatre were captivated by sketches like the modern version of the Good Samaritan set on a train travelling from, 'London to York, London to York, London to York.'

With this background, it is strange to own up to the fact that I have wrestled a great deal with the very concept of first-person narrative sermons. By their very nature they are profoundly dramatic and, when well done; they captivate the imagination in a profoundly personal way. Yet, I struggle with the concept, even though it closely parallels the way I have used drama in worship throughout my ministry.

I initially came across first-person narrative preaching in the United States where Haddon Robinson and Paul Borden spoke warmly of its impact and effectiveness as a medium for communication with a congregation. Respecting their experience and insight I first put my difficulties down to a cultural peculiarity tied up with that British sense of reserve and the formal sense of the dignity of the pulpit. But that was not it. This was not my starting point at all. It was only later that I made the connection with acting. Maybe my instinctive reactions had something to do with acting and the role of the preacher.

My mature reflections have only confirmed and deepened this conviction. In many ways, as preachers we perform every time we stand up to preach the gospel. Yet in performing the function of the preacher it must never become a performance. A wise mentor said to me while I was still a young and inexperienced preacher, 'When you preach, always be yourself and always preach from your own Christian experience.' I have always tried to do that.

Professor Richard M. Perloff of the Department of Communication at Cleveland State University talks about the 'source credibility' of any communication. He maintains that the credibility of the communicator is probably the oldest of all concepts in persuasion theory, tracing it back to Aristotle who held that the character of the speaker was the most effective means of persuasion anyone possesses.[2] I concluded that this was where my problem lay. If first-person narrative sermons require me to take on the role of another, then, of necessity I am acting. Not that acting in a worship service is wrong, far from it. No, it is because I am acting as a preacher. The raison d'être of preaching is to communicate the truth of the Word of God. Yet, if the preacher is consciously acting the whole process is open to the charge of simply 'being an act' and therefore fundamentally undermining the credibility of the preacher.

Does this mean that first-person narrative sermons ought to be off-limits to the preacher? It would be easy and logical to argue that on this basis. Yet, preachers who are greatly respected wordsmiths of the gospel, whose integrity is beyond reproach find first-person narrative to be a genre that powerfully speaks God's truth into people's lives. Maybe my wrestling says more about me and the temptation I have to resist of drawing on my experience and acting ability to improve my preaching beyond the reality of who I am before God and thereby turn it into mere acting. There is a thin line between preaching and acting. It is a line that is easy to cross and we do well to be aware of its existence and make sure that we do not cross it.

A friend asked me why I was writing a book for preachers on such an esoteric subject. It got me thinking. From what you have read you will understand why I think that this particular form of preaching has much to offer us. However, as

---

[2] Perloff, *Dynamics of Persuasion*, 137–8.

I thought about my friend's question I began to reflect on our attitude as preachers to our calling. Underlying my passion as a preacher to see the Word of God effectively communicated to our generation sits a desire to be the best preacher that I can be.

Some years ago I did a course at CTVC, the churches television centre, on effective communication. Roy Trevivian was co-leader of the programme of study. During a review of material we had produced he spoke with intense conviction about never being prepared to settle for second best as we speak for Jesus. 'This is the Word of Life,' he said, 'not just some meaningless and throwaway conversation!' A seed was sown in that comment that has grown into an ongoing conviction for me about our attitudes as preachers to the task we undertake. I believe strongly that:

- We should always be ready to learn more and have our understanding deepened and our horizons broadened in our practice of preaching.
- We should always be prepared to change and adapt what we do and not stagnate into the comfortable habits of our past experience. Habits that can suffocate the spiritual vitality of our preaching and cause us to fail to engage with the radical living reality testified to in the Scriptures.
- We should always be open to the cultural context within which we minister, so that our communication of the timeless Word of God might be contextually tailored to specifically fit the people we address.

A while ago I was leading a day conference for an Anglican Diocese in the middle of England. Three dozen lay readers joined me to explore preaching in a narrative style one Saturday. At the end of the afternoon a lady in her fifties came to thank me. Her eyes sparkled and she was clearly very excited. 'Thank you for today', she said, 'you've helped me to understand what it is that I've been doing in my preaching recently. I love telling the stories to our congregation. It's so exciting as a preacher to let the Lord lead you into doing things differently for him and to see his Word come alive for people so that they get enthusiastic about it too!'

If this is where preaching in a narrative style leads you then I will be a happy man. Then, for once, we really will be finding the plot rather than losing it!

12

Going Further

There are many resources that you can access if you are interested in exploring narrative preaching further, developing your preaching skills or merely discovering more material to assist you.

BOOKS

Narrative preaching
Robert Alter, *The Art of Biblical Narrative* (New York: Basic Books, 1981)
> *An introduction to the genre of biblical narratives from a Jewish perspective. More of an academic than an homiletical work.*

Jana Childers, *Performing the Word: Preaching as Theatre* (Nashville: Abingdon Press, 1998)
> *Looks at what preachers can learn from the stage and seeks to destigmatise a performance based approach to preaching.*

J. Kent Edwards, *Effective First-Person Biblical Preaching: the Steps From Text to Narrative Sermon* (Grand Rapids: Zondervan, 2005)
> *J. Kent Edwards is Professor of Preaching & Leadership at Talbot School of Theology in California. Here he develops Haddon Robinson's 'big idea' into a step-by-step guide to first person narrative preaching. The book contains example sermons and a CD-Rom with video content.*

David A Enyart, *Creative Anticipation: Narrative Sermon Designs for Telling the Story* (Philadelphia: Xlibris, 2002)
Explores the nature of narrative and how to "plot" a sermon to benefit from the advantages of narrative structure.

Richard L Eslinger, *Narrative Imagination* (Minneapolis: Fortress Press, 1995)
Eslinger is an American Methodist and his writing reflects that background. The book is split into theory and practice with sample sermons have a commentary in parallel.

Reg Grant & John Reed, *Telling Stories to Touch the Heart* (Wheaton: Victor Books, 1990)
Focuses on presentation, and the basics of how can improve our preaching style to tell stories better.

Mike Graves & David J. Schlafer (eds.), *What's the Shape of Narrative Preaching? Essays in Honor of Eugene L. Lowry* (Saint Louis: Chalice Press, 2008)
An edited book of essays can often be of variable quality. In this volume writing by leading teachers and practitioners in homiletics the standard is consistently high. Ronald Allen addresses the different views of narrative preaching while Robin Meyers compares narrative preaching to performing Jazz.

Sidney Greidanus, *The Modern Preacher and the Ancient Text: Interpreting and Preaching Biblical Literature* (Leicester: IVP, 1988)
An excellent book, if a little detailed, to help you connect your preaching with the style and forms of Scripture. This book has become a contemporary classic.

Richard A Jensen, *Thinking in Story: Preaching in a Post-Literate Age* (Lima: CSS, 1993)
Jensen is a stimulating writer who will compel you to think through the issues of preaching in our time. Not a long book, but it will challenge you to engage with why you do what you do.

David L Larsen, *Telling the Old, Old Story: The Art of Narrative Preaching* (Grand Rapids: Kregel, 1995)

This is a thoughtful overview of the subject from an experienced pastor, preacher and homiletics tutor at Trinity Evangelical Divinity School. Larsen will take you further with his thorough and readable contribution.

Richard Littledale, *Stale Bread? a Handbook for Speaking the Story* (Edinburgh: Saint Andrew Press, 2007)

An English Baptist pastor and broadcaster, Littledale sees the use of storytelling and narrative preaching as part of wider strategy to refresh the preacher's art. While the book is initially a little confusing as he talks about preaching in the first, second and third voice rather than the more common usage of first and third person preaching, this book is well worth reading.

Eugene Lowry, *The Homiletical Plot: The Sermon as Narrative Art Form* (Atlanta: John Knox Press, 1980)

Eugene Lowry, *How to Preach a Parable: Designs for Narrative Sermons* (Nashville: Abingdon, 1989)

These books are not to be missed for preachers interested in narrative preaching. Lowry's work is the foundational to the genre and is essential reading for those wanting to explore it more fully.

Thomas G. Long, *Preaching and the Literary Forms of the Bible* (Philadelphia: Fortress Press, 1989)

Long's book is a key text covering similar ground to Greidanus, but is a shorter and more demanding read. While only one chapter specifically addresses preaching on narratives, this is a stimulating and rewarding text.

Steven D. Mathewson, *The Art of Preaching Old Testament Narrative* (Grand Rapids: Baker, 2002)

Not for the faint hearted, this is a PhD thesis turned into a book. However, it is a very comprehensive treatment and also has five sample sermons, one from Haddon Robinson, who also writes the foreword.

David Mulder, *Narrative Preaching: Stories from the Pulpit* (St. Louis: Concordia, 1996)

Written to stimulate sermon preparation, this slim volume briefly explores various kinds of narrative preaching that the author identifies with accompanying sample sermons to illustrate his observations.

Richard L. Pratt, *He Gave Us Stories: The Bible Students Guide to Interpreting Old Testament Narratives* (Phillipsburg: P & R Publishing, 1993)
Concentrates solely on OT narratives and how the preacher can use them.

Haddon W. Robinson & Torrey W. Robinson, *It's All in How You Tell It: Preaching First-Person Expository Messages* (Grand Rapids, Baker Books, 2003)
An excellent page introduction to preaching in the first-person style with seven example sermons and an appendix of where to find resource material.

Narrative theory

H. Porter Abbott, *The Cambridge Introduction to Narrative* (Cambridge: CUP, 2008)
Interacting with the different genres of narrative in contemporary Western culture, Abbot demonstrates how narrative is constructed, how it acts upon us, how it is transmitted etc. This is an excellent place to start if you are interesting in understanding the theory more adequately.

Peter Abbs & John Richardson, *The Forms of Narrative: A practical study guide for English* (Cambridge: CUP, 1990)
A very readable and accessible introduction to narrative designed for High School students. It explores the stories themselves, the component parts that comprise the essential elements to narrative, the different ways stories can be told and the various types and genres of narrative that might be encountered.

Mieke Bal, *Narratology: Introduction to the Theory of* Narrative 3rd ed. (Toronto: University of Toronto Press, 2009)
First published in , this book has become one of the standard introductions on the theory of narrative texts. 'Narratology' is the study of how such narratives are brought into being; the dynamics that make them work and how they are received and understood.

Paul Cobley, *Narrative* (London: Routledge, 2001)
A comprehensive historic overview of narrative from Aristotle to the cinema, cyberspace and postmodernism.

Robert Fulford, *The Triumph of Narrative: Storytelling in the Age of Mass Culture* (New York: Broadway, 2001)
Fulford's book is a readable exploration of contemporary trends in narrative and our need for stories in our lives by a Canadian broadcaster and journalist.

Jack Hart, *Storycraft: The Complete Guide to Writing Narrative Nonfiction* (Chicago: University of Chicago Press, 2011)
While written from a journalistic perspective, Hart looks to see how communicating nonfiction can be more effective by using the tools of narrative construction, ie, the structure (narrative arc) of exposition, crisis, resolution, and denouement, and the same elements - theme, character, scene. A readable and insightful window into professional, nonfiction narrative communication.

David Herman, Manfred Jahn & Marie-Laure Ryan (eds.), *Routledge Encyclopedia of Narrative Theory* (London: Routledge, 2007)
A helpful and informative introduction to all the ideas, concepts and language that the industry of storytelling has thrown up, helpfully organised in the classic A-Z form of an encyclopedia.

Jakob Lothe, *Narrative in Fiction and Film: An Introduction* (Oxford: OUP, 2000)
Divided into two part, the former introduces the key concepts of narrative while the latter five texts (including Mark's gospel, Franz Kafka and Virginia Woolf) and the movie versions of four of them.

Noah Lukeman, *The Plot Thickens: Ways to Bring Fiction to Life* (New York, 2002)
Lukeman is a literary agent and uses his experience of professionally dealing with thousands of pitches for new books each year to analyse the classic ingredients to storytelling and what makes them work.

Brian Richardson (ed.), *Narrative Dynamics: Essays on Time, Plot, Closure, and Frames* (Columbus: The Ohio State University Press, 2002)
An anthology of twenty-seven essays exploring the core ingredients that result in a good narrative. While it is not of consistent quality the excerpts are drawn from impressive sources including E.M. Forster and Jacques Derrida.

Michael Toolan, *Narrative: a critical linguistic introduction, second edition* (London: Routledge, 2001)
An academic at Britain's University of Birmingham, Toolan explores the component parts of narrative and what systematic attention to language can reveal about the narrative itself, the storyteller and those to whom a story is addressed.

Contemporary issues in preaching

Ronald Allen, Barbara Blaisdell & Scott Johnson, *Theology for Preaching: Authority, Truth, and Knowledge of God in a Postmodern Ethos* (Nashville, Abingdon, 1997)
This book seeks to engage with the challenges of postmodernism head-on through theological dialogue together around the homiletic task. A very stimulating read with refreshing conclusions.

Martyn Atkins, *Preaching in a Cultural Context* (Peterborough: Foundary Press, 2001)
Atkins explores what preaching will look like as it changes to address our new cultural milieu. Rather than being negative about the changes that are happening around us, he sees many things to be positive finding ways for the postmodern themes of pluralism, relativism and the rejection of metanarratives to become strengths.

Robert G Duffett, *A Relevant Word: Communicating the Gospel to Seekers* (Valley Forge: Judson Press, 1995)
An excellent volume that explores the issues involved in making sermons more "seeker sensitive".

Mike Graves (ed.), *What's the Matter with Preaching Today?* (Louisville; London: Westminster John Knox, 2004)

A stimulating book of contributions from gifted preaching practitioners who identify a range of challenges that confront contemporary preachers and offer helpful suggestions to enable those charged with the responsibility for preaching to begin to address them.

Graham Johnson, Preaching *to a Postmodern World: A Guide to Reaching Twenty-First Century Listeners* (Grand Rapids: Baker Books, 2001)

A more general book about contemporary preaching, but fast becoming a highly regarded text. It does what it says on the cover.

Craig Loscalzo, *Preaching Sermons That Connect* (Downers Gove: IVP, 1992)

Craig Loscalzo, *Evangelistic Preaching That Connect* (Downers Gove: IVP, 1995)

Loscalzo is an experienced preacher and teacher of preachers. He believes that every sermon has to win a hearing. His passion is to see preachers connect with their listeners through identification and "becoming one with them".

Doug Pagitt, *Preaching in the Inventive Age* (Minneapolis: Sparkhouse, 2011)

In an 'open source' world, Pagitt shares how a practice of 'progressional dialogue' has developed at Solomon's Porch, Minneapolis to become an inclusive and participatory form of communication.

Michael Rogness, *Preaching to a TV Generation* (Lima: CSS, 1994)

This may be a slim book, but it is creative and stimulating book that seeks to identify how we respond to the challenge of a culture saturated with electronic media. It contains my favourite all-time quote on the need to have culturally relevant preaching that compares using our received traditions of preaching with showing old black and white movies in a Dolby Surround Sound multiplex of today!

Geoffrey Stevenson (ed.), *The Future of Preaching* (London: SCM, 2010)

Writing from the conviction that preaching has future, fourteen contributors reflect on what that might look like from a British perspective.

Thomas Troeger, *Ten Strategies for Preaching in a Multi Media Culture* (Nashville: Abingdon, 1996)

This is a book that you will either love or hate. Troeger is keen to explore new strategies to make preaching more engaging for the listener. However much some of is suggestions may sit uncomfortably with the reader, they will certainly make you think through what you do.

Timothy A. Turner, *Preaching to a Programmed People: Effective Communication in a Media-Saturated Society* (Grand Rapids: Kregel, 1995)

Given that television is the all-pervading influence in our society Turner seeks to understand what it has done to its audience and how that needs to impact us as preachers.

Preaching and communication

David Buttrick, *Homiletic: Moves and Structures* (Philadelphia: Fortress Press, 1987)

A major book on the theory and construction of sermons, Preaching Magazine described this text "… the most encyclopaedic work in the modern period."

Fred B. Craddock, *Preaching* (Nashville: Abingdon, 1985)

This book was written to be a standard textbook for those in training for ministry. It is comprehensive, informative and thorough in its approach weaving history, theology and hermeneutics into a practical and helpful text for the preaching practitioner.

David Day, Jeff Astley & Leslie J. Francis (eds.), *A Reader on Preaching: Making Connections* (Aldershot: Ashgate, 2005)

A series of articles from a range of international teachers and practitioners. Practically rooted and yet theoretically informed, this volume strategically covers the principles, processes, context and theology of preaching.

Michael Duduit, *The Handbook of Contemporary Preaching* (Nashville: Broadman Press, 1992)

This is a series of articles on many different aspects of preaching. It is a great general resource to help you understand and develop your preaching. It is a text that I would not want to be without and also contains a good chapter on narrative preaching by Calvin Miller.

Calvin Miller, *The Empowered Communicator: Keys to Unlocking an Audience* (Nashville: Broadman Press, 1994)

Calvin Miller, *Spirit, Word and Story: A Philosophy of Marketplace Preaching* (Grand Rapids: Baker Books, 1996)

Calvin Miller, *The Sermon Maker: Tales of a Transformed Preacher* (Grand Rapids: Zondervan, 2003)

Miller is a former pastor, a prolific author and is presently professor of preaching and pastoral ministry at Samford University's Beeson Divinity School in Birmingham, Alabama. The three titles above indicate the direction of this highly-regarded and well-loved writer when he writes about preaching. First and foremost he writes as a pastor-practitioner.

Michael J. Quicke, -*Degree Preaching: Hearing, Speaking, and Living the Word* (Grand Rapids: Baker Books, 2003)

This is a standard preaching textbook for the twenty-first century that is comprehensive, refreshing and insightful. Michael Quicke is presently Professor of Preaching and Communication at Northern Baptist Seminary in Illinois having previously served as Principal of Spurgeon's College in London.

Michael J. Quicke, *Preaching as Worship: an Integrative Approach to Formation in Your Church* (Grand Rapids: Baker Books, 2011)

The relationship between worship and preaching is important to understand. Here they are seen as functioning organically and holistically together to both honor the persons of the Godhead and play their part in community formation.

Haddon W. Robinson, *Expository Preaching* (IVP, 2001)

The most widely-used and hugely-respected textbook for Expository Preaching in the USA. While Robinson does not touch on narrative preaching in this text, he believes the principles of "BIG IDEA" preaching are to be applied in exactly the same way when taking a narrative approach. This is a new and thoroughly revised edition of his classic work Biblical Preaching.

Haddon W. Robinson, *Biblical Sermons* (Baker Books, 1989)

Contains sample sermons of preachers and an analysis of each alongside an interview with the preacher.

Geoffrey Stevenson & Stephen Wright, *Preaching with Humanity: a Practical Guide for Today's Church* (London: Church House, 2008)

Acknowledging the humanity of both the preacher and the congregation this book examines the various contexts of preaching - mission, worship, education and pastoral care - along with the various 'players' in the sermon - beginning with God and ending with the preacher themselves - before looking at the practical issues of preparation and delivery.

John Stott, *I believe in Preaching* (London: Hodder & Stoughton, 1982)

Stott is perhaps the most highly regarded British preacher for a generation. In this volume of the "I believe …" series he ranges comprehensively over the whole subject of preaching. He includes the theological foundations of preaching, its objectives and an apologetic in the wake of contemporary scepticism. Alongside these he tackles the need to study and the practice of preparation and delivery.

Warren Wiersbe, *Preaching & Teaching with Imagination* (Wheaton: Victor Books, 1994)

Wiersbe's commentaries easy-to-read and insightful commentaries sit on many preachers' bookshelves and are often quarried for their insights into the biblical text and their anecdotes from life. In this book Wiersbe contends that preachers have analysed the Scriptures to death resulting in "skeletons in the pulpit and cadavers in the pew"! He pleads for more imagination, life and vitality.

Keith Willhite & Scott M Gibson (eds.), *The Big Idea of Biblical Preaching* (Baker Books, 1998)
This volume is dedicated to Haddon Robinson and is an apologetic for the "Big Idea" approach to preaching that he has advocated. It contains an excellent chapter by Paul Borden on narrative preaching.

Stephen Wright, *Alive to the Word: a Practical Theology of Preaching for the Whole Church* (London: SCM, 2010)
An informed and substantive introduction to preaching that draws on the insights and developments in homiletics over the last quarter of a century. It places preaching in the context of its basic theological rationale right through to the dynamics of live communication and the necessary development of the preacher's spirituality, understanding and skill.

OTHER RESOURCES

United Kingdom

The College of Preachers is an Anglican-based fellowship of lay and ordained preachers. The College seeks to train and resource preachers through its journal, day training conferences and annual gathering. A distance learning qualification that is offered at post-graduate level has been developed in conjunction with Spurgeon's College in London.
<www.collegeofpreachers.org.uk>
<www.spurgeons.ac.uk>

The Expository Times is a monthly periodical that seeks to combine an interest in pastoral matters with the latest international biblical and theological scholarship. It consists of approximately 30,000 words per issue.
<http://ext.sagepub.com/>

The Proclamation Trust was founded by Dick Lucas in 1986 and runs conferences and training courses for preachers. Drawing on the services of keys leaders like Dick Lucas and

Don Carson, the Trust is committed to effectively teach the Bible to preachers so that they can in turn teach it to others. <www.proctrust.org.uk>

United States

The Evangelical Homiletics Society was formed in 1997 and consists mostly of homiletics professors. Their website carries some very interesting papers from their annual conferences. <www.ehomiletics.com/>

Homiletics Journal is a periodical that includes biblical commentary, illustrations, children's sermons, articles and worship ideas. **Homiletics Online** is the web-based sister of Homiletics journal and has over 10 years worth of weekly instalments pulled from the journal. It is a subscription service. An iPad app is also available. <www.homileticsonline.com>

The Academy of Homiletics is an association of some 400 members. They produce their own journal, Homiletic, and maintain a website with good onward links. <homiletics.org>

Preaching Magazine is a bi-monthly periodical designed to encourage and enhance the ministry of those who are called to preach. With contributions from experienced and highly regarded exponents of preaching each issue contains practical feature articles, a selection of model sermons, and a helpful group of homiletical resources including "From the Lectionary," "To Illustrate," "The Preacher's Bookshelf," and "The Back Page Pulpit". <www.preaching.com>

Courses of study in homiletics are far more widely available in the United States than the United Kingdom. Contact your nearest seminary to find out what might be on offer. A helpful list of accredited seminaries can be obtained from the Association of Theological Schools in the United States and Canada who have around 250 schools in association with them. <www.ats.edu>

Internet based material

Online Pulpit This is an online blog that is part of the IVP family. Drawing on the insights of working pastors and authors its aim is to provide a diversity of perspective and practice with the aim of equipping preachers for their task.
<http://onlinepulpit.ivpress.com/>

Preaching.com is the web service of 'Preaching' magazine and contains many more resources including articles, illustrations, an on-line bookstore and a free weekly newsletter delivered by email that you can sign up for.
<www.preaching.com>

www.sermons.com has been operation since 1997, beginning as a single website it has grown to a network of sites (including Sermons.com, eSermons.com, ChildrensSermons.com, ChildrensBulletins.org, SermonIllustrations.com, ChurchMail.com, BiblicalArcheology.com, Clergy.net, Lectionary.net, Christian-Dramas.com, and more) providing resources for sermon and worship development. Leonard Sweet of Drew Theological School is the chief writer for this site.
<www.sermons.com>

Day1 began its life as the radio broadcast, 'The Protestant Hour' in 1945 and has been on the airwaves every week since, presently taken by over 200 stations. Its online site has an extensive range of videos, podcasts and transcripts from contributors from the mainline Protestant denominations including the Cooperative Baptist Fellowship, the Episcopal Church, Evangelical Lutheran Church in America, Presbyterian Church (U.S.A.), United Church of Christ, and the United Methodist Church. The material is lectionary based.
<http://day1.org>

PreachingToday.com is probably the most comprehensive preaching resource available on the internet. Run by the Christianity Today organisation, its subscription service gives access to a large, searchable database of illustrations, articles, sermons (audio and transcripts) etc. There is also a free weekly newsletter delivered by email that you can sign up for.

Sermonwriter.com is a range of lectionary based sermon resources available on subscription. The website is service by Dick Donovan, a former homiletics officer for the US Army Chaplaincy.

<www.sermonwriter.com>

Christian Ethereal Library contains classic Christian books in electronic format, all believed to be in the public domain and therefore free in pdf or plain text formats. Apple iBooks and Amazon Kindle version are available, although these will incur a charge. There is enough good reading material here to last you a lifetime.

<www.ccel.org>

Desperatepreacher.com is a predominantly Anglican subscription site. However, it carries a vast array of resources, idea, materials for the desperate preacher including an online community discussion forum.

<http://desperatepreacher.com>

SermonCentral claims to be the largest sermon research site in the world. Over 120,000 sermons, videos, PowerPoints, illustrations, and other material are available for subscribers, with free resources also accessible for the casual visitor to the site.

<www.sermoncentral.com>

The African American Pulpit is the online version of a quarterly printed periodical.

<www.theafricanamericanpulpit.com>

Willow Creek Association carries a large amount of resources from the international network that has grown around the ministry of Bill Hybels and the church at the South Barrington Church, Illinois. These include Bible studies, messages, dramas, curriculum and books which are all available via their on-line store. There is also news of conferences and a great deal more.

<www.willowcreek.com>

<www.willowcreek.org.uk>

Bibliography

Abbott, H. Porter, *The Cambridge Introduction to Narrative* (Cambridge: Cambridge University Press, 2002)

Abbs, Peter & John Richardson, *The Forms of Narrative: A Practical Guide* (Cambridge: Cambridge University Press, 1990)

Alter, Robert, *The Art of Biblical Narrative* (New York: Basic Books 1981)

Anderson, Leith, *A Church for the 21st Century* (Minneapolis: Bethany, 1992)

Babin, Pierre, *The New Era in Religious Communication* (tr. David Smith; Minneapolis: Fortress Press, 1991)

Bailey, Kenneth E., *Poet and Peasant: A Literary-cultural Approach to the Parables in Luke* (Grand Rapids: Eerdmans, 1976)

—, *Through Peasant Eyes: More Lucan Parables, Their Culture and Style* (Grand Rapids: Eerdmans, 1980)

Barna, George, *Generation Next: What You Need to Know About Today's Youth* (Ventura: Regal, 1995)

Bosch, David J., *Transforming Mission: Paradigm Shifts in Theology of Mission* (New York: Orbis, 1991)

Brierley, Peter, *UK Christian Handbook* (London: HarperCollins. 1999)

Bronte, Charlotte, *Jane Eyre* (London: W. Nicholson & Sons, nd)

Brooks, Peter, *Reading for the Plot: Design and Intention in Narrative* (Oxford: Clarendon Press, 1984)

Brooks, Phillips, *Eight Lectures on Preaching* (5th edn.; London: SPCK, 1879; reprinted 1959)

Clements, Roy, 'Expository Preaching in a Postmodern World', *Cambridge Papers* 7:3 (September 1998)

Cobley, Paul, *Narrative* (London: Routledge, 2001)

Coupland, Douglas, *Generation X* (London: Abacus, 1992)

Craddock, Fred B., *As One Without Authority: Essays on Inductive Preaching* (Nashville: Abingdon Press, 1971)

—, *Overhearing the Gospel* (Nashville: Abingdon Press, 1978)

Cray, Graham (ed.), *The Post Evangelical Debate* (London: Triangle, 1997)

Davis, H. Grady, *Design for Preaching* (Philadephia: Fortress Press, 1958)

Dixon, Patrick, *Futurewise: Six Faces of Global Change* (London: HarperCollins, 1998)

Duduit, Michael (ed.), *Handbook of Contemporary Preaching* (Nashville: Broadman Press, 1992)

Eslinger, Richard L., *Narrative Imagination: Preaching the Worlds That Shape Us* (Minneapolis: Fortress Press, 1995)

Ford, Kevin G., *Jesus for a New Generation: Reaching Out to Today's Young Adults* (Downers Grove: InterVarsity Press, 1995)

Forster, E.M., *Aspects of the Novel* (New York: Harcourt Brace, 1927)

Fulford, Robert, *The Triumph of Narrative: Storytelling in the Age of Mass Media* (New York: Broadway Books, 2000)

Grant, Reg and John Reed, *Telling Stories to Touch the Heart* (Wheaton: Victory Books, 1990)

Greidanus, Sidney, *The Modern Preacher and the Ancient Text: Interpreting and Preaching Biblical Literature* (Leicester: Inter-Varsity Press, 1988)

Guinness, Os, *Dining with the Devil: The Megachurch Movement Flirts with Modernity* (Grand Rapids: Baker Book House, 1993)

—, *Fit Bodies, Fat Minds: Why Evangelicals Don't Think and What to Do About It* (Grand Rapids: Baker Book House, 1994)

Guinness, Os and John Seel (eds.), *No God but God* (Chicago: Moody Press, 1992)

Hauerwas, Stanley and L. Gregory Jones (eds.), *Why Narrative?: Readings in Narrative Theology* (Grand Rapids: Eerdmans, 1989)

Hilborn, David, *Picking Up the Pieces: Can Evangelicals Adapt to Contemporary Culture?* (London: Hodder & Stoughton, 1997)

Jensen, Richard A., *Thinking in Story* (Lima OH: CSS, 1993)

Klein, William W., Craig L. Blomberg & Robert L. Hubbard, *Introduction to Biblical Interpretation* (Dallas: Word, 1993)

Larsen, David L., *Telling the Old, Old Story: The Art of Narrative Preaching* (Grand Rapids: Kregel, 1995)

Larson, Charles U., *Persuasion: Reception and Responsibility* (Belmont: Wadsworth, 1998)

Long, Thomas G., *Preaching and the Literary Forms of the Bible* (Philadelphia: Fortress Press, 1989)

Lothe, Jakob, *Narrative in Fiction and Film: An Introduction* (Oxford: Oxford University Press, 2000)

Lowry, Eugene L., *The Homiletical Plot: The Sermon as Narrative Art Form* (Atlanta: John Knox Press, 1980)

Lukeman, Noah, *The Plot Thickens* (New York: St Martin's Press, 2002)

Miller, Calvin, *Spirit, Word, and Story: A Philosophy of Marketplace Preaching* (Grand Rapids: Baker Book House, 1996)

Mouw, Richard J., *Consulting the Faithful: What Christian Intellectuals Can Learn from Popular Religion* (Grand Rapids: Eerdmans, 1994)

Perloff, Richard, *The Dynamics of Persuasion* (New Jersey: Lawrence Eltbaum Associates, 1993)

Postman, Neil, *Amusing Ourselves to Death: Public Discourse in the Age of Show Business* (New York: Penguin, 1985)

Pritchard, Gregory, *Willow Creek Seeker Services* (Grand Rapids: Baker Book House, 1996)

Richardson, Brian (ed.), *Narrative Dynamics: Essays on Plot, Time, Closure, and Frames* (Columbus: The Ohio State University Press, 2002)

Robinson, Haddon W., *Biblical Preaching: The Development and Delivery of Expository Messages* (Grand Rapids: Baker Book House, 1980)

—, *Expository Preaching: Its Principles and Practice* (Leicester: Inter-Vrasity Press, 2001)

Robinson, Haddon W. & Torrey W. Robinson, *It's All in How You Tell It: Preaching First-person Expository Messages* (Grand Rapids: Baker Book House, 2003)

Rogness, Michael, *Preaching to a TV Generation* (Lima OH: CSS, 1994)

Roof, Wade C., *A Generation of Seekers: The Spiritual Journeys of the Baby Boom Generation* (New York: HarperCollins, 1993)

Sontag, Susan, *A Barthes Reader* (New York: Hill and Wang, 1982)

Stott, John, *Between Two Worlds: The Art of Preaching in the Twentieth Century* (Grand Rapids: Eerdmans, 1982)

Tomlinson, Dave, *The Post Evangelical* (London: Triangle, 1995)

Toolan, Michael, *Narrative: A Critical Linguistic Introduction* (London: Routledge, 2001)

Troeger, Thomas H., *Ten Strategies for Preaching in a Multimedia Culture* (Nashville: Abingdon, 1996)

Turner, Timothy A., *Preaching to Programmed People: Effective Communication in a Media-saturated Society* (Grand Rapids: Kregel, 1995)

Walker, Andrew, *Telling the Story: Gospel, Mission and Culture* (London: SPCK, 1996)

Warner, Rob, *21st Century Church: (Why Radical change Cannot Wait)* (London: Hodder & Stoughton, 1994)

Watson, David, *You are my God* (London: Hodder & Stoughton, 1983)

Wells, David, *No Place for Truth* (Grand Rapids: Eerdmans, 1994)

Willhite, Keith & Scott M. Gibson, *The Big Idea of Biblical Preaching* (Grand Rapids: Baker Book House, 1998)

Wicker, Brian, *The Story-Shaped World: Fiction and Metaphysics: Some Variations on a Theme* (London: Athlone Press, 1975)

Zimbardo, Philip G. and Michael R. Leippe, *The Psychology of Attitude Change and Social Influence* (Boston: McGraw Hill, 1991)

Scripture Index

Author Index

Lightning Source UK Ltd.
Milton Keynes UK
UKOW051125061112

201749UK00010B/114/P

9 781620 320310